Implications of the Reykjavik Summit on Its Twentieth Anniversary

CONFERENCE REPORT

The Hoover Institution gratefully acknowledges

THE LYNDE AND HARRY BRADLEY FOUNDATION
THE HONORABLE ROBERT D. STUART JR.

for their significant support of the conference
Implications of the Reykjavik Summit
on Its Twentieth Anniversary
and this resultant publication.

Implications of the Reykjavik Summit on Its Twentieth Anniversary

CONFERENCE REPORT

Conference Organizers
and Report Editors:
*Sidney D. Drell and
George P. Shultz*

Conference held
October 11–12, 2006
at the Hoover Institution,
Stanford University

HOOVER INSTITUTION
Stanford University
Stanford, California

The Hoover Institution on War, Revolution and Peace, founded
at Stanford University in 1919 by Herbert Hoover, who went on
to become the thirty-first president of the United States, is an
interdisciplinary research center for advanced study on domestic
and international affairs. The views expressed in its publications are
entirely those of the authors and do not necessarily reflect the views
of the staff, officers, or Board of Overseers of the Hoover Institution.

www.hoover.org

Hoover Institution Press Publication No. 558

First printing, 2007
14 13 12 11 10 09 08 07   9 8 7 6 5 4 3 2 1

Manufactured in the United States of America

The paper used in this publication meets the minimum requirements
of the American National Standard for Information Sciences
Permanence of Paper for Printed Library Materials, ANSI Z39.48-1992. ∞

Library of Congress Cataloging-in-Publication Data
Implications of the Reykjavik summit on its twentieth anniversary : conference
report / conference organizers and report editors, Sidney D. Drell and George P.
Shultz.
     p.   cm. — (Hoover Institution Press publication ; no. 558)
  "Conference held October 11–12, 2006 at the Hoover Institution, Stanford
University."
  Includes bibliographical references and index.
  ISBN-13: 978-0-8179-4841-2 (cloth: alk. paper)
  ISBN-13: 978-0-8179-4842-9 (pbk.: alk. paper)
1. Nuclear nonproliferation—Congresses. 2. United States—Foreign relations—
Soviet Union—Congresses. 3. Soviet Union—Foreign relations—United States—
Congresses. 4. United States—Foreign relations—1981–1989—
Congresses. 5. Summit meetings—Iceland—Reykjavìk—Congresses. 6. Visits
of state—Iceland—Reykjavìk—Congresses. 7. Reagan, Ronald—Congresses.
8. Gorbachev, Mikhail Sergeevich, 1931–   —Congresses. I. Drell, Sidney D.
(Sidney David), 1926–   II. Shultz, George Pratt, 1920–   III. Hoover
Institution on War, Revolution and Peace. IV. Title. V. Series.
JZ5675.I67 2007
327.1'747—dc22   2007037502

Contents

Appendix One: Memorandum of Conversation
(Transcript of the discussions of President Ronald
Reagan and Secretary of State George P. Shultz with
General Secretary Mikhail Gorbachev and Foreign

Preface

We have talked together a lot about issues of arms control and about the devastating consequences of a nuclear explosion. *The Gravest Danger*, by Sid Drell and Jim Goodby, with a Foreword by George Shultz, addresses this issue.

Out of all this discussion came the idea of holding a conference on the twentieth anniversary of the meeting in Reykjavik between President Reagan and General Secretary Gorbachev. The idea was not so much to rehash the Reykjavik events as to talk about the implications of what was discussed there.

We are very pleased that the idea attracted a group of outstanding people, and the discussion for all of us was genuinely rewarding. At its conclusion, Bill Perry suggested that we should have a follow-up meeting, and we plan to organize one.

In the meantime, we have put together in this little booklet some of the extraordinary material presented to the conference. Also included is an op-ed piece that was a derivative of the conference and that appeared in the *Wall Street Journal* on January 4, 2007. The reactions to this piece have been generally favorable, so we are encouraged to continue working at this project. We were particularly struck by a letter from Mikhail Gorbachev, which is also included in this booklet.

George P. Shultz   *Sidney D. Drell*

Related
Newspaper
Articles

A World Free of Nuclear Weapons

George P. Shultz,
William J. Perry,
Henry A. Kissinger,
and Sam Nunn

NUCLEAR WEAPONS TODAY present tremendous dangers, but also an historic opportunity. U.S. leadership will be required to take the world to the next stage—to a solid consensus for reversing reliance on nuclear weapons globally as a vital contribution to preventing their proliferation into potentially dangerous hands, and ultimately ending them as a threat to the world.

Nuclear weapons were essential to maintaining international security during the Cold War because they were a means of deterrence. The end of the Cold War made the doctrine of mutual Soviet-American deterrence obsolete. Deter-

Mr. Shultz, a distinguished fellow at the Hoover Institution at Stanford, was secretary of state from 1982 to 1989. Mr. Perry was secretary of defense from 1994 to 1997. Mr. Kissinger, chairman of Kissinger Associates, was secretary of state from 1973 to 1977. Mr. Nunn is former chairman of the Senate Armed Services Committee.

A conference organized by Mr. Shultz and Sidney D. Drell was held at the Hoover Institution to reconsider the vision that Reagan and Mr. Gorbachev brought to Reykjavik. In addition to Messrs. Shultz and Drell, the following participants also endorse the view in this statement: Martin Anderson, Steve Andreasen, Michael Armacost, William Crowe, James Goodby, Thomas Graham Jr., Thomas Henriksen, David Holloway, Max Kampelman, Jack Matlock Jr., John McLaughlin, Don Oberdorfer, Rozanne Ridgway, Henry Rowen, Roald Sagdeev and Abraham Sofaer.

This commentary originally appeared in the *Wall Street Journal* on January 4, 2007, page A15.

rence continues to be a relevant consideration for many states with regard to threats from other states. But reliance on nuclear weapons for this purpose is becoming increasingly hazardous and decreasingly effective.

North Korea's recent nuclear test and Iran's refusal to stop its program to enrich uranium—potentially to weapons grade—highlight the fact that the world is now on the precipice of a new and dangerous nuclear era. Most alarmingly, the likelihood that nonstate terrorists will get their hands on nuclear weaponry is increasing. In today's war waged on world order by terrorists, nuclear weapons are the ultimate means of mass devastation. And non-state terrorist groups with nuclear weapons are conceptually outside the bounds of a deterrent strategy and present difficult new security challenges.

Apart from the terrorist threat, unless urgent new actions are taken, the U.S. soon will be compelled to enter a new nuclear era that will be more precarious, psychologically disorienting, and economically even more costly than was Cold War deterrence. It is far from certain that we can successfully replicate the old Soviet-American "mutually assured destruction" with an increasing number of potential nuclear enemies worldwide without dramatically increasing the risk that nuclear weapons will be used. New nuclear states do not have the benefit of years of step-by-step safeguards put in effect during the Cold War to prevent nuclear accidents, misjudgments, or unauthorized launches. The United States and the Soviet Union learned from mistakes that were less than fatal. Both countries were diligent to ensure that no nuclear weapon was used during the Cold War, by design or by accident. Will new nuclear nations and the world be as fortunate in the next 50 years as we were during the Cold War?

* * *

LEADERS ADDRESSED THIS issue in earlier times. In his "Atoms for Peace" address to the United Nations in 1953, Dwight D. Eisenhower pledged America's "determination to help solve the fearful atomic dilemma—to devote its entire heart and mind to find the way by which the miraculous inventiveness of man shall not be dedicated to his death, but consecrated to his life." John F. Kennedy, seeking to break the logjam on nuclear disarmament, said, "The world was not meant to be a prison in which man awaits his execution."

Rajiv Gandhi, addressing the U.N. General Assembly on June 9, 1988, appealed, "Nuclear war will not mean the death of a hundred million people. Or even a thousand million. It will mean the extinction of four thousand million: the end of life as we know it on our planet Earth. We come to the United Nations to seek your support. We seek your support to put a stop to this madness."

Ronald Reagan called for the abolishment of "all nuclear weapons," which he considered to be "totally irrational, totally inhumane, good for nothing but killing, possibly destructive of life on Earth and civilization." Mikhail Gorbachev shared this vision, which had also been expressed by previous American presidents.

Although Reagan and Mr. Gorbachev failed at Reykjavik to achieve the goal of an agreement to get rid of all nuclear weapons, they did succeed in turning the arms race on its head. They initiated steps leading to significant reductions in deployed long- and intermediate-range nuclear forces, including the elimination of an entire class of threatening missiles.

What will it take to rekindle the vision shared by Reagan and Mr. Gorbachev? Can a worldwide consensus be forged that defines a series of practical steps leading to major reductions in the nuclear danger? There is an urgent need to address the challenge posed by these two questions.

The Non-Proliferation Treaty (NPT) envisioned the end of all nuclear weapons. It provides (a) that states that did not possess nuclear weapons as of 1967 agree not to obtain them, and (b) that states that do possess them agree to divest themselves of these weapons over time. Every president of both parties since Richard Nixon has reaffirmed these treaty obligations, but non-nuclear weapon states have grown increasingly skeptical of the sincerity of the nuclear powers.

Strong non-proliferation efforts are under way. The Cooperative Threat Reduction program, the Global Threat Reduction Initiative, the Proliferation Security Initiative, and the Additional Protocols are innovative approaches that provide powerful new tools for detecting activities that violate the NPT and endanger world security. They deserve full implementation. The negotiations on proliferation of nuclear weapons by North Korea and Iran, involving all the permanent members of the Security Council plus Germany and Japan, are crucially important. They must be energetically pursued.

But by themselves, none of these steps are adequate to the danger. Reagan and General Secretary Gorbachev aspired to accomplish more at their meeting in Reykjavik 20 years ago—the elimination of nuclear weapons altogether. Their vision shocked experts in the doctrine of nuclear deterrence, but galvanized the hopes of people around the world. The leaders of the two countries with the largest arsenals of nuclear weapons discussed the abolition of their most powerful weapons.

* * *

WHAT SHOULD BE DONE? Can the promise of the NPT and the possibilities envisioned at Reykjavik be brought to fruition? We believe that a major effort should be launched by the United States to produce a positive answer through concrete stages.

First and foremost is intensive work with leaders of the

countries in possession of nuclear weapons to turn the goal of a world without nuclear weapons into a joint enterprise. Such a joint enterprise, by involving changes in the disposition of the states possessing nuclear weapons, would lend additional weight to efforts already under way to avoid the emergence of a nuclear-armed North Korea and Iran.

The program on which agreements should be sought would constitute a series of agreed and urgent steps that would lay the groundwork for a world free of the nuclear threat. Steps would include:

- Changing the Cold War posture of deployed nuclear weapons to increase warning time and thereby reduce the danger of an accidental or unauthorized use of a nuclear weapon.

- Continuing to reduce substantially the size of nuclear forces in all states that possess them.

- Eliminating short-range nuclear weapons designed to be forward-deployed.

- Initiating a bipartisan process with the Senate, including understandings to increase confidence and provide for periodic review, to achieve ratification of the Comprehensive Test Ban Treaty, taking advantage of recent technical advances, and working to secure ratification by other key states.

- Providing the highest possible standards of security for all stocks of weapons, weapons-usable plutonium, and highly enriched uranium everywhere in the world.

- Getting control of the uranium enrichment process, combined with the guarantee that uranium for nuclear power reactors could be obtained at a reasonable price, first from the Nuclear Suppliers Group and then from the International Atomic Energy Agency (IAEA) or other controlled international reserves. It will also be necessary to deal with proliferation issues presented by spent fuel from reactors producing electricity.

• Halting the production of fissile material for weapons globally; phasing out the use of highly enriched uranium in civil commerce; and removing weapons-usable uranium from research facilities around the world and rendering the materials safe.

• Redoubling our efforts to resolve regional confrontations and conflicts that give rise to new nuclear powers.

Achieving the goal of a world free of nuclear weapons will also require effective measures to impede or counter any nuclear-related conduct that is potentially threatening to the security of any state or peoples.

Reassertion of the vision of a world free of nuclear weapons and practical measures toward achieving that goal would be, and would be perceived as, a bold initiative consistent with America's moral heritage. The effort could have a profoundly positive impact on the security of future generations. Without the bold vision, the actions will not be perceived as fair or urgent. Without the actions, the vision will not be perceived as realistic or possible.

We endorse setting the goal of a world free of nuclear weapons and working energetically on the actions required to achieve that goal, beginning with the measures outlined above.

The Nuclear Threat

Mikhail Gorbachev

THE ESSAY "A World Free of Nuclear Weapons," published in this newspaper on Jan. 4, was signed by a bipartisan group of four influential Americans—George Shultz, William Perry, Henry Kissinger, and Sam Nunn—not known for utopian thinking and having unique experience in shaping the policies of previous administrations. It raises an issue of crucial importance for world affairs: the need for the abolition of nuclear weapons.

As someone who signed the first treaties on real reductions in nuclear weapons, I feel it is my duty to support their call for urgent action.

The road to this goal began in November 1985 when Ronald Reagan and I met in Geneva. We declared that "a nuclear war cannot be won and must never be fought." This was said at a time when many people in the military and among the political establishment regarded a war involving weapons of mass destruction as conceivable and even acceptable, and were developing various scenarios of nuclear escalation.

It took political will to transcend the old thinking and attain a new vision. For if a nuclear war is inconceivable, then mil-

Mr. Gorbachev was the leader of the Soviet Union from 1985 to 1991.

This commentary originally appeared in the *Wall Street Journal* on January 31, 2007, page A13.

itary doctrines, armed forces development plans, and negotiating positions at arms-control talks must change accordingly.
This began to happen, particularly after Reagan and I agreed
in Reykjavik in October 1986 on the need ultimately to eliminate nuclear weapons. Concurrently, major positive changes
were occurring in world affairs: A number of international
conflicts were defused and democratic processes in many parts
of the world gained momentum, leading to the end of the Cold
War.

As U.S.-Soviet arms negotiations got off the ground, a
breakthrough was achieved—the treaty on the elimination of
medium- and shorter-range missiles, followed by agreement
on 50% reduction in strategic offensive weapons. If the negotiations had continued in the same vein and at the same pace,
the world would have been rid of the greater part of the arsenals of deadly weapons. But this did not happen, and hopes
for a new, more democratic world order were not fulfilled. In
fact, we have seen a failure of political leadership, which
proved incapable of seizing the opportunities opened by the
end of the Cold War. This glaring failure has allowed nuclear
weapons and their proliferation to pose a continuing, growing
threat to mankind.

The ABM Treaty has been abrogated; the requirements for
effective verification and irreversibility of nuclear-arms reductions have been weakened; the treaty on comprehensive cessation of nuclear-weapons tests has not been ratified by all
nuclear powers. The goal of the eventual elimination of nuclear weapons has been essentially forgotten. What is more,
the military doctrines of major powers, first the United States
and then, to some extent, Russia, have re-emphasized nuclear
weapons as an acceptable means of war fighting, to be used
in a first or even in a "pre-emptive" strike.

All this is a blatant violation of the nuclear powers' commitments under the Non-Proliferation Treaty. Its Article V is clear and unambiguous: Nations that are capable of making nuclear weapons shall forgo that possibility in exchange for the promise by the members of the nuclear club to reduce and eventually abolish their nuclear arsenals. If this reciprocity is not observed, then the entire structure of the treaty will collapse.

The Non-Proliferation Treaty is already under considerable stress. The emergence of India and Pakistan as nuclear-weapon states, the North Korean nuclear program, and the issue of Iran are just the harbingers of even more dangerous problems that we will have to face unless we overcome the present situation. A new threat, nuclear weapons falling into the hands of terrorists, is a challenge to our ability to work together internationally and to our technological ingenuity. But we should not delude ourselves: In the final analysis, this problem can only be solved through the abolition of nuclear weapons. So long as they continue to exist, the danger will be with us, like the famous "rifle on the wall" that will fire sooner or later.

Last November, the Forum of Nobel Peace Laureates, meeting in Rome, issued a special statement on this issue. The late Nobel laureate and world-renowned scientist, Joseph Rotblat, initiated a global awareness campaign on the nuclear danger, in which I participated. Ted Turner's Nuclear Threat Initiative provides important support for specific measures to reduce weapons of mass destruction. With all of them we are united by a common understanding of the need to save the Non-Proliferation Treaty and of the primary responsibility of the members of the nuclear club.

We must put the goal of eliminating nuclear weapons back on the agenda, not in a distant future but as soon as possible. It links the moral imperative—the rejection of such weapons from an ethical standpoint—with the imperative of assuring security. It is becoming clearer that nuclear weapons are no longer a means of achieving security; in fact, with every passing year they make our security more precarious.

The irony—and a reproach to the current generation of world leaders—is that two decades after the end of the Cold War the world is still burdened with vast arsenals of nuclear weapons of which even a fraction would be enough to destroy civilization. As in the 1980s, we face the problem of political will—the responsibility of the leaders of major powers for bridging the gap between the rhetoric of peace and security and the real threat looming over the world. While agreeing with the Jan. 4 article that the United States should take the initiative and play an active role on this issue, I believe there is also a need for major efforts on the part of Russian and European leaders and for a responsible position and full involvement of all states that have nuclear weapons.

I am calling for a dialogue to be launched within the framework of the Nuclear Non-Proliferation Treaty, involving both nuclear-weapon states and non-nuclear-weapon states, to cover the full range of issues related to the elimination of those weapons. The goal is to develop a common concept for moving toward a world free of nuclear weapons.

The key to success is reciprocity of obligations and actions. The members of the nuclear club should formally reiterate their commitment to reducing and ultimately eliminating nuclear weapons. As a token of their serious intent, they should without delay take two crucial steps: ratify the comprehensive test ban treaty and make changes in their military doctrines, removing nuclear weapons from the Cold War–era high alert status. At the same time, the states that have nuclear-power programs would pledge to terminate all elements of those programs that could have military use.

The participants in the dialogue should report its progress and the results achieved to the United Nations Security Council, which must be given a key coordinating role in this process.

Over the past 15 years, the goal of the elimination of nuclear weapons has been so much on the back burner that it will take a true political breakthrough and a major intellectual effort to achieve success in this endeavor. It will be a challenge to the current generation of leaders, a test of their maturity and ability to act that they must not fail. It is our duty to help them to meet this challenge.

Papers
Prepared
for the
Conference

President Reagan's Nuclear Legacy

James E. Goodby

RONALD REAGAN'S LEGACY includes four lines of thought that were roundly criticized in his day, but that still challenge us to think afresh about our nuclear dilemmas. They are:

- an emphasis on the ultimate futility of dependence on nuclear weapons for national security;
- a paradigm shift from arms control, as practiced since the early 1960s, to nuclear disarmament;
- ballistic missile defense as a key to reductions in strategic offensive forces;
- the *de facto* termination of a nuclear war fighting doctrine known as "protracted nuclear war."

Futility of Nuclear War

"Let Reagan be Reagan," some of the president's political supporters urged, when they thought his advisers were hemming him in too much. In Reykjavik, Reagan really was Reagan. President Reagan was appalled by the catastrophic damage that a nuclear war would inflict. He called mutual assured destruction (MAD) "uncivilized." Even before he became president, as governor of California, he had visited Lawrence Livermore National Laboratory and other national security

James Goodby is a Research Fellow at the Hoover Institution. He has served as a career diplomat with rank of Ambassador on a number of arms control and nonproliferation negotiations. His most recent book is *At the Borderline of Armageddon: How American Presidents Managed the Bomb* (Rowman and Littlefield, 2006).

facilities. His abhorrence of nuclear weapons was genuine and consistent for many years.

After Reykjavik, in a question-and-answer session with media representatives on December 11, 1987, he said, "For a number of years, before I ever got here, I have been concerned about the very presence of nuclear weapons. . . ." On the same occasion, alluding to his partner in nuclear negotiations, Mikhail Gorbachev, Reagan said, "To hear this man now, without any urging from me, express his wish that we could totally eliminate nuclear weapons because of the threat they represent—and he quoted back to me a line I used as long ago as 1982. . . . 'A nuclear war cannot be won and must never be fought.' "

Could this have been posturing for political advantage? Not at all. These were sentiments he voiced very often, and not only in public. In an Oval Office meeting with the president in 1985, he said to me: "You tell people that I'm willing to go as far as anyone else in getting rid of nuclear weapons." I asked Paul Nitze once whether Reagan really meant what he said about nuclear weapons. His answer was that in his experience Reagan was more like Harry Truman than any other president: each man said exactly what he thought.

A Shift Away from Arms Control

The "summer study" conducted in Cambridge, Massachusetts in 1960 led to the theory of "arms control" that eventually replaced the older idea of disarmament. The purpose of arms control as defined by Thomas Schelling and Morton Halperin was ". . . all the forms of military cooperation between potential enemies in the interest of reducing the likelihood of war, its scope and violence if it occurs, and the political and economic costs of being prepared for it." Whether arms control should involve reductions or increases in certain kinds of military force was treated as an open question.

Arms control was a success: nuclear weapons were not used in anger after 1945. Its guiding principles influenced defense planning during a succession of U.S. administrations. Its central tenets—for example, that a "firebreak" should be maintained between nuclear and conventional forces—are valid today. But arms control was relatively indifferent to the levels of forces, except in the context of preserving a secure retaliatory nuclear strike. To Reagan, this seemed to be a fatal defect. For a leader who thinks of MAD as "uncivilized," arms negotiations should be about reductions, not about how best to control a nuclear buildup. He expressed this thought many times. His remarks on October 14, 1986, in which he recalled his thinking on the subject, capsulized the way he viewed the issue: ". . . our objective . . . must not be regulating the growth in nuclear weapons, which is what arms control, as it was known, had been all about. . . . our goal must be reducing the number of nuclear weapons . . . we had, to work to make the world safer, not just control the pace at which it became more dangerous."

This is why Reykjavik was about nuclear reductions and about the goal of eliminating nuclear weapons and not about "arms control" as it had evolved since the 1960s. And this, of course, is why Reagan opted for the "zero option" in intermediate-range nuclear forces (INF) and for deep reductions in strategic nuclear forces.

This departure from arms control bothered people who were steeped in the ideas of classical arms control theory. In the winter of 1985, even before Reykjavik, Schelling wrote that "nobody ever offers a convincing reason for preferring smaller numbers. . . . If people really believe that zero is the ultimate goal it is easy to see that downward is the direction they should go. But hardly anyone who takes arms control seriously believes that zero is the goal." After Reykjavik, Senator Al Gore Jr. praised some of its achievements, but said of the ideas about eliminating offensive forces: "Here we depart from arms control for the less charted waters of disarmament." Gore's aim was strategic stability, and he said that this should be pursued "not through complete disarmament on short notice, but through arms control."

Reagan's ideas prevailed, partly because the end of the Cold War made such ideas more popular. Deep reductions were pursued by his successor, George H. W. Bush, who completed the Strategic Arms Reduction Talks (START) I treaty and negotiated a START II treaty. President Bill Clinton sought a START III treaty with still deeper reductions. President George W. Bush concluded a U.S.-Russian treaty that ratified ceilings of 1,700 to 2,200 operationally deployed warheads on each side.

Reagan may not have foreseen the utility of deep reductions in nuclear weapons as a nonproliferation tool in an age of terrorism. But it is a fact that classical arms control offered few incentives to nonnuclear weapons states to remain that way. And nuclear deterrence, which arms control sought to stabilize, has little or no effect on terrorists. Now, it is clear that Reagan's ideas about nuclear weapons are directly responsive to the political needs of governments that might be inclined to forgo nuclear weapons. Reagan's philosophy was at the core of the nonproliferation bargain between the nuclear "haves" and "have nots."

Ballistic Missile Defense As a
Key to Elimination of Nuclear Weapons

Reagan was not the first president to support the elimination of nuclear weapons. That idea emerged in the Acheson-Lillienthal proposals, which became the Baruch Plan. Harry

Truman backed it. Nor was Reagan the first president to support ballistic missile defense. Lyndon Johnson reluctantly made the decision to deploy ballistic missiles and actually did so. But Reagan was the first president to think and to argue that ballistic missile defense would permit deep reductions in offensive nuclear forces and ultimately make possible the elimination of nuclear weapons. "SDI [Strategic Defense Initiative] is the key to a world without nuclear weapons," he said in his report on Reykjavik on October 13, 1986. He explained this by saying that "having the defense would protect against cheating or the possibility of a madman sometime deciding to create nuclear missiles."

Nitze elaborated on the idea and wrote about "defense dominance," the idea that defensive capabilities could ultimately be more powerful as a deterrent than offensive forces. In a speech he gave on February 20, 1985, he said that

> during the next ten years, the U.S. objective is a radical reduction in the power of existing and planned offensive nuclear arms, as well as the stabilization of the relationship between offensive and defensive nuclear arms, whether on earth or in space. We are even now looking forward to a period of transition to a more stable world, with greatly reduced levels of nuclear arms and an enhanced ability to deter war based upon an increasing contribution of nonnuclear defenses against offensive nuclear arms. This period of transition could lead to the eventual elimination of all nuclear arms, both offensive and defensive. A world free of nuclear arms is an ultimate objective to which we, the Soviet Union, and all other nations can agree.

Reagan, of course, realized that his vision could not be achieved through U.S. efforts alone. For this reason he sought a treaty with the Soviet Union that would bring down the numbers of offensive weapons on each side. Equally important, he proposed technological cooperation with Moscow so that both sides could deploy defensive systems. This was the only formula, he realized, that would enable "defense dominance" to be achieved.

The Attack on the Theory of "Protracted Nuclear War"

As the Soviet Union and the United States entered a condition that amounted to parity in strategic nuclear forces, each side intensified its search for methods to eke out advantages. In the United States, this led first to limited nuclear options and eventually to the idea that a nuclear war might be fought incrementally through a series of strikes against the enemy's military and industrial assets. Nitze, ever in the vanguard of deterrent theory, was one of the leading proponents of this doctrine. He wrote that the United States needed "something on the order of 3,000 deliverable megatons remaining in reserve after a counter-force exchange" to deter the Soviet Union.

Zbigniew Brzezinski, President Carter's national security adviser, was instrumental in making protracted nuclear war an official part of U.S. strategic doctrine. This was recorded in Presidential Directive-59 of July 25, 1980. This is what Ronald Reagan inherited when he took office, and he reportedly endorsed it early in his administration.

Reagan believed that the Soviet Union had taken a dangerous lead in strategic nuclear forces. Indeed, indicators such as number of warheads and throw-weight suggested that. His first move was to correct what he saw as an imbalance in the U.S.-Soviet nuclear relation in favor of Moscow. Had his presidency ended in 1985, his time in office would have been seen as a time of rapid buildup in U.S. nuclear forces. Protracted nuclear war requires high numbers of warheads, and Reagan's buildup would have been consistent with that doctrine. But in his second term, as dramatized at Reykjavik, Reagan pushed hard for lower levels of nuclear forces. This policy made it more difficult to implement the doctrine of protracted nuclear war and meant, for practical purposes, a turn away from the doctrine he had inherited.

When I began my service as vice chairman of the U.S. START I delegation, I found from my talks with my Soviet counterparts that they were thinking about and planning for an agreement that would permit several thousand nuclear warheads. This, indeed, was the trend that both sides had come to accept as a normal part of maintaining deterrence in an era of protracted nuclear war. Reagan did not see this as a state of affairs that should be continued.

In time, the end of the Cold War made the doctrine of a U.S.-Soviet protracted nuclear war obsolete. But Reagan had already started down that road when he decided that arms control was not enough and that U.S. policy should go in the direction of eliminating nuclear weapons.

Nuclear Weapons Elimination: A Process

Thomas Graham Jr.

PAUL NITZE WAS the archetypical Cold Warrior and nuclear weapon strategist. As the author of National Security Council Report 68, commissioned by President Harry Truman in 1950, he helped set the ground rules for the Cold War and the thermonuclear confrontation. However, nearly fifty years later, in the last op-ed that he wrote at the age of 92 in 1999 entitled "A Danger Mostly to Ourselves," he said:

> I know that the simplest and most direct answer to the problem of nuclear weapons has always been their complete elimination.

Senator Sam Nunn, in an article in the *Financial Times* in December 2004, pointed to the immense danger that exists as a result of the fact that fifteen years after the end of the Cold War, the United States and Russia still maintain, on fifteen minutes alert, long-range strategic missiles equipped with immensely powerful nuclear warheads capable of devastating each other's societies in thirty minutes. In 1995, Russia mistook the launch of a test rocket in Norway for a submarine-launched nuclear missile aimed at Moscow and came within two minutes of ordering a retaliatory nuclear strike on the

Ambassador Thomas Graham Jr. participated in a senior capacity in every major arms control/nonproliferation negotiation involving the U.S. from 1970 to 1997. Currently he is Chairman of the Board of Directors of the Cypress Fund for Peace and Security and an adjunct professor at the University of Washington, Seattle.

United States. Senator Nunn said in his article that our current nuclear weapon policy, which in effect relies on the deteriorating Russian early warning system's continuing to make correct judgments as it did during the Cold War, "risks an Armageddon of our own making."

And former Defense Secretary William Perry, a scientist not given to exaggeration, said not long ago that in his judgment there could be a greater than 50 percent chance of a nuclear detonation on U.S. soil in the next decade.

The Nuclear Non-Proliferation Treaty (NPT) is the centerpiece of world security. President John F. Kennedy truly feared that nuclear weapons might well sweep all over the world. In 1962, there were reports that by the late 1970s there could be twenty-five to thirty nuclear weapon states in the world, with nuclear weapons integrated into their arsenals. If that had happened, there would be many more such states today than there actually are—in September 2004, the director general of the International Atomic Energy Agency (IAEA), Mohamed El Baradei, estimated that more than forty countries had the capability to build nuclear weapons. Under such conditions, every conflict would carry with it the risk of going nuclear, and it would be impossible to keep nuclear weapons out of the hands of international terrorist organizations, they would be so widespread.

But such weapon proliferation did not happen, and the principal reason that it did not was the negotiation of the NPT and its entry into force in 1970, buttressed by the policies of extended nuclear deterrence—the nuclear umbrella—followed by the United States and the Soviet Union with their Cold War Treaty Allies. Indeed since 1970 until now, there has been very little nuclear weapon proliferation. In addition to the five nuclear weapon states recognized by the NPT (the United States, Britain, France, Russia, and China), three states (India, Pakistan, and Israel, and perhaps North Korea) have built nuclear weapon arsenals (but India and Israel were already well along in 1970). This is far from what President Kennedy feared.

But the success of the NPT was no accident. It was rooted in a carefully crafted central bargain. In exchange for a commitment from the nonnuclear weapon states (today more than 180 nations, most of the world) not to acquire nuclear weapons and to submit to international safeguards to verify compliance with this commitment, the NPT nuclear weapon states pledged unfettered access to peaceful nuclear technologies and undertook to engage in nuclear disarmament negotiations aimed at the ultimate elimination of their nuclear arsenals. It is this basic bargain that for the last three decades has formed the central underpinnings of the international nonproliferation regime.

However, one of the principal problems with all this has been that the nuclear weapon states have never really delivered on the disarmament part of this bargain, and the United States in recent years appears to have largely abandoned it.

And now the other side of the bargain has begun to fall apart. India and Pakistan eroded the NPT from the outside by each conducting a series of nuclear weapon tests in 1998 and declaring themselves to be nuclear weapon states. India, Pakistan, and Israel maintain sizable unregulated nuclear weapon arsenals outside the NPT. North Korea withdrew from the NPT in 2003 and may have built as many as eight or nine nuclear weapons. Whereas the new agreement with North Korea is promising, elimination of this possible arsenal is far in the future. The secret and illegal A. Q. Khan nuclear weapon technology transferring ring based in Pakistan has been exposed, but who can be sure that this is but the tip of the iceberg? Iran is suspected of having a nuclear weapon program and admitted in late 2003 that contrary to its IAEA safeguards agreement, it failed to report its acquisition of uranium enrichment technology. The Iranian case appears to be growing more serious and has become a major international issue. However, the threat is long-term, not immediate. Military action against Iran is not the answer; rather it is patient, careful diplomacy. To quote a comment by Zbigniew Brzezinski: "I think of war with Iran as the ending of America's present role in the world." Hopefully, the resumption of the negotiations between the European Union and Iran, with the United States participating, will lead to a solution.

And why might Iran want the nuclear fuel cycle and the attendant option to construct nuclear weapons? The nuclear program is very popular in Iran. It appears that some countries believe that ultimately the only way that they can gain respect in this world, as President Lula of Brazil declared during his first election campaign, is to acquire nuclear weapons. During the Cold War, nuclear weapons distinguished "great powers" from others countries. The permanent members of the Security Council are the five recognized nuclear weapon states. Forty years ago, Great Britain and France both asserted that status was the real reason they were building nuclear weapons. India declared in 1998 that it was now a big country, it had nuclear weapons. This high political value of nuclear weapons has not changed since the Cold War.

In view of all this, it is of paramount importance to attempt to revive the NPT as a treaty system based on law and to restore its credibility. A first and probably essential step would be to bring into force the Comprehensive Nuclear Test Ban Treaty. Other urgent and far-reaching steps would be required. However, we must recognize that it may now simply be too late to attempt to change the course of nations and return to policies that will strengthen and support the NPT and the international nonproliferation regime. The NPT does not have the support today that it had in the past. In the context of a breakdown of world order and the war on terror, with the potential failure of the NPT and the ensuing likelihood of the widespread nuclear proliferation that President Kennedy so rightly feared many years ago and with nuclear tension a growing threat with thousands of strategic nuclear weapons still on high alert and a Russian early warning system continuing to decline in effectiveness, there is a real possibility that it is too late for nuclear arms limitation. In the interest of the security and safety of us all, perhaps a way must be found to proceed directly to the elimination of nuclear weapons, as Nitze suggested more than seven years ago.

How could nuclear weapons actually be eliminated? A possible course of action could be for the president of the United States to call for an extraordinary session of the United Nations General Assembly and ask to address the Assembly. In his speech, the president could call for the worldwide elimination of nuclear weapons (as well as all other weapons of mass destruction) and request that the Security Council be charged to carry out this task. The Security Council could then call for the negotiation of a treaty to eliminate nuclear weapons. This would require worldwide intrusive onsite inspection and probably security guarantees to a number of states on the edge of conflicts and where nuclear programs are or may be present, such as Israel, Iran, Pakistan, and North Korea. North Korea would return to the NPT as a nonnuclear weapon state. There would need to be an agreement by all states to apply economic and, if necessary, military pressure to any state that did not comply with this program or that subsequently violated the negotiated arrangements. In an interim stage, the five NPT nuclear weapon states and the three other longtime holdouts from the NPT would be required to remove all nuclear weapons from alert status and then to eliminate almost all of their arsenals, bringing them down to very low levels. A second and later stage would require elimination of weapons but for these eight states, which would be allowed to keep a relatively limited amount of nuclear explosive material (highly enriched uranium or plutonium) that could be converted into a small number of weapons as a hedge. This could amount to roughly enough material for five weapons each for India, Pakistan, and Israel, fifteen weapons each for Britain, France, and China and thirty weapons each for the United States and Russia. The material would be maintained under very high levels of national security protection at designated depositories and would also be under international safeguards implemented by IAEA inspectors. Under various programs, all other nuclear explosive material would be eliminated worldwide. Nuclear power production would be reconfigured so as to make no more plutonium, by the use of nonproliferative fuels and advanced reactors. The plutonium in existing spent nuclear fuel around the world would have to be eliminated as well. Such an arrangement would take a long time to negotiate and even longer to implement—but we must try, for the hour is late. A final stage, years in the future, could be the verifiable elimination of the fissile material retained by the eight nuclear states, but only after the issue of "missing" fissile material, a feature of the nuclear weapon inventories in probably all of the nuclear weapon states, has been effectively addressed.

Some might say that this is unrealistic. How could we ever hope that the U.S. government, or any other government possessing a nuclear arsenal, would even contemplate such a thing? I would say in response that we must press for and hope for the best and remember that nothing good is ever impossible. Who would have thought that the zero intermediate-range nuclear forces missile option proposed by President Reagan in 1981 would ever happen? Who would have thought the

Cold War would end in the foreseeable future? Who would have thought the Soviet Union would cease to exist? But all of these things did happen.

However, in order to achieve the elimination of nuclear weapons and to establish a peaceful and secure world community in the twenty-first century, the United States must lead—there is no alternative. But for this to happen, the United States must be believed and trusted. On September 12, 2001, the United States had the trust and support of the entire world. Now that support and trust is gone, and the United States is reviled and feared in many quarters of the world. Senator John McCain said a few months ago that "America's position in the world is at an all-time low." How can we regain the trust of the world community? How can we return to our historic destiny of keeping the peace and fostering the development of the community of nations, democracies, free market economies, the international rule of law, international institutions, and treaty arrangements?

Among other things we should:

First, recognize that in the wake of the Cold War, the world has fundamentally changed: the nation state system that has dominated international life for the last 350 years is rapidly deteriorating. Perhaps some fifty to seventy nations around the world are inexorably slipping into the category of failed states. We cannot go it alone. Poverty, disease, cultural misunderstandings, and machine-gun societies around the world are central national security threats; these are the principal causes of international terrorism. The primary weapons in the battle against terror and a declining world order are economic, political, social, cultural and diplomatic, and only rarely military.

And second, for more than fifty years the United States pursued a world order built on rules and international treaties that permitted the expansion of democracy and the enlargement of international security. In April 2005, in a speech before the American Society of International Law, the secretary of state said that when the United States respects its "international legal obligations and supports an international system based on the rule of law, we do the work of making this world a better place, but also a safe and more secure place for America." We should take such steps as ratifying the Comprehensive Nuclear Test Ban Treaty, joining the Ottawa Land Mine Convention, becoming a part of the International Criminal Court, and in general, establishing ourselves again as strong advocates of the international rule of law.

In this way we can regain our historic role, and we can and we will effectively lead the world community to a safe, secure, stable and just twenty-first century.

The Legacy of Reykjavik: Preserving a Security Option for Dealing with Madmen, Missiles, and Missile Defense

Thomas H. Henriksen

"We should have some way of defending ourselves against nuclear missiles."

—Ronald Reagan, July 31, 1979*

"I think we had a reasonable chance of shooting it down."

—George W. Bush, July 7, 2006, in response to a question about North Korea's launch of its Taepodong 2 missile three days earlier†

THE FORTUNATE LEGACY of the Reykjavik Summit lies in wisdom of the American delegation to preserve the option for a missile defense system. Twenty years after the landmark meeting in Iceland, the world is witnessing a plenitude of missile threats, a key, if not *the central*, motif at the Soviet-American parley. The thunderstorm of rocket firings from Lebanon to North Korea in 2006 makes it clear that the missile menace did not expire with the Soviet Union. The projectiles launched by the

Thomas H. Henriksen is a Senior Fellow at the Hoover Institution. His current reseach focuses on American foreign policy in the post–Cold War world. His most recent book is *American Power After the Berlin Wall* (Palgrave Macmillan, 2007).

*Cited in Martin Anderson, *Revolution: The Reagan Legacy* (Stanford, California, Hoover Institution Press, 1990), page 83.

† Quoted from the President's White House Press Briefing, July 7, 2006. Downloaded: http://www.whitehouse.gov/news/releases/2006/07/print/20060707-1.html

North Koreans and Hezbollah alert mankind to the very real prospect that even more frightening payloads will exist in the next-generation missiles. The apprehension of missile warfare has not receded in the twenty years since Soviet-American negotiators met to discuss nuclear disarmament and missile defense in Reykjavik.

The Defense of Missile Defense

Nuclear-tipped missiles—and a possible defensive shield—were uppermost in the minds of the Soviet-American delegations at Reykjavik. Even before taking office, President Ronald Reagan wanted to defend against incoming nuclear missiles. In his 1983 speech that publicly announced the Strategic Defense Initiative (SDI), Reagan committed the United States to the search for a strategic missile defense system. This novel American approach soon encountered stiff Soviet opposition to what Moscow termed "space-strike weapons."

Two salient facts about America's commitment to an antimissile system stand out from the pivotal 1986 summit.[1] First and foremost, Reagan did not regard the SDI as a bargaining chip in the crucial negotiations with the Soviet Union's Mikhail Gorbachev.[2] President Reagan pressed hard to convince the Soviet general secretary about the necessity of a defense against nuclear-armed ballistic missiles for both the United States of America and the Union of Soviet Socialist Republics. The Kremlin chief was wedded to the status quo in the strategic construct as set forth in the 1972 Anti-Ballistic Missile

1. For a vivid and authoritative account of the Reykjavik summit, see George P. Shultz, *Turmoil and Triumph: My Years As Secretary of State* (New York: Charles Scribner's Sons, 1993), pages 751–80.
2. A description of the evolution of the Strategic Defense Initiative up to Ronald Reagan's announcement speech to the nation on March 23, 1983, can be found in Anderson, *Revolution*, pages 80–99.

Treaty, which enshrined the notion of mutual assured destruction (MAD) for both signatories if nuclear war were to break out. In the arms control calculus, MAD represented the ultimate stable deterrent against a Soviet nuclear attack, for Moscow risked joint destruction with the United States. President Reagan argued that in the event of a Soviet inter-continental ballistic missile (ICBM) attack, the MAD strategy left the United States with the unpalatable decision of either doing nothing against a barrage of long-range nuclear missiles or retaliating in kind against Moscow. He hated the choices.

At the historic Soviet-American meeting in Iceland, Ronald Reagan argued for the elimination of all ballistic missiles, for he had long held an especial distaste for the thought of a thermonuclear war. Capitalizing on this apprehension, the Soviet leader offered his U.S. counterpart what seemed the deal of the twentieth century—the reduction of both sides' strategic offensive arms over a ten-year period to achieve total elimination. But Gorbachev's proposal contained a catch that remained a deal breaker. The Kremlin chief wanted Reagan to halt all testing in space of new SDI technologies, confining research and testing on SDI technologies to the laboratory. The Soviet leader never defined what he meant by a laboratory, but his intent was to keep the SDI from going into operation.

In response to this sweeping proposal, Ronald Reagan asked: "If we both eliminate nuclear weapons, why would there be a concern if one side wants to build defensive systems just in case?"[3] Trying to forge an agreement, America's fortieth commander-in-chief even offered to share SDI technology with the Soviet Union. But he and his secretary of state, George Shultz, would not renounce SDI, believing that without it they had "no leverage to propel the Soviets to continue moving our

3. Shultz, *Turmoil and Triumph*, page 771.

way."[4] The Reagan foreign policy team held firm on sustaining research and development on an antimissile system for strategic long-range ballistic missiles at Reykjavik, despite the immediate perception by the media and pundits of a monumental diplomatic failure on the subarctic island. These first impressions judged that the United States had walked away from an array of Soviet concessions because of a dubious Star Wars fantasy.

Without "SDI as an ongoing propellant," in the words of George Shultz, Moscow's arms control "concessions could wither away over the next ten years."[5] As the secretary of state and others realized, without the SDI impetus there was no reason for their opposite numbers to come to the negotiating table. As it turned out, during the subsequent George H. W. Bush administration, Gorbachev did, in fact, enter into sweeping nuclear arms reductions in the Strategic Arms Reduction Talks with the United States that had been furthered by the Reagan administration's stance. Had Reagan bargained away the prospects and promise of some type of defense-based deterrence system, it would have been the greatest one-sided bad bargain since Esau sold his birthright to Jacob for bread and pottage. Killing the concept of a defensive option to the MAD strategy would have increased the vulnerability that confronts the United States in the post–Cold War era.

The second and other significant Reykjavik factor that looms large today is that Reagan saw beyond focusing on just the Soviet Union as the only target for his proposed missile defense. It is true that President Reagan strove to eliminate nuclear weapons. But his passion for a protective defense system against strategic ballistic missiles encompassed a much

4. Ibid., page 773.
5. Ibid., page 775.

wider scope than just the Soviet Union. In a March 1988 speech, nearly two years after Reykjavik, he asserted: "People who put their trust in MAD must trust it to work 100 percent forever—no slip-ups, no madmen, no unmanageable crises, no mistakes—forever."[6]

Madman and SDI

Before exploring the vindication of President Reagan's post-Soviet view, it is important to note his thinking on the uses of a missile defense system. Even before Reykjavik, he envisioned the SDI as protection against not only the Soviet Union but also other threats. After his 1983 speech inaugurating the SDI, Reagan faced accusations that he simply employed a stratagem, or bargaining chip, to compel the Soviets to reduce their nuclear armory. He argued otherwise to American and Soviet listeners. Later, Reagan wrote with unusual prescience: "One day a madman could come along and make the missiles and blackmail all of us—but not if we have a defense against him."[7]

President Reagan saw the SDI, not as an "impenetrable shield—no defense could ever be expected to be 100 percent effective," but, as he later wrote, as "a safety valve against cheating—or attacks by lunatics who managed to get their hands on a nuclear missile."[8]

Reagan desperately wanted to reach a verifiable agreement with the Soviets before, after, and during Reykjavik to eliminate nuclear weapons by year 2000, as Gorbachev proposed in early 1986, ten months before the Icelandic summit. What gave the U.S. chief executive officer serious pause were worries

6. Quoted from Paul Lettow, *Ronald Reagan and His Quest to Abolish Nuclear Weapons* (New York: Random House, 2005), page 240.

7. Ronald Reagan, *An American Life* (New York: Simon and Schuster, 1990), page 548.

8. Ibid., page 608.

about an SDI-less America. Such a defenseless scenario left the United States vulnerable, even naked, to long-range strategic missile threats. The ABM treaty did permit tactical and air defense–type missiles.

In his autobiography, the former president wrote a rhetorical question to his readers about the passing of nuclear-tipped missiles into the wrong grasp: "What about the Qaddafis of the world or a lunatic who got his hands on an A-bomb?"[9]

In mentioning by name Muammar al-Qaddafi, the Libyan strongman and terrorist mastermind of a rash of bombings and murders from the 1970s through the downing of Pan Am Flight 103 over Lockerbie, Scotland, in December 1988, Reagan farsightedly identified the type of threat America would face in the post-Soviet period. By resorting to terrorism and defying the international community, Qaddafi was the quintessential rogue dictator of the past era. Later, even more wicked and violent men displaced him as terrorist chieftains or took the reins of government in Afghanistan, Iraq, Iran, and North Korea.

Just as Reagan wanted to trust but verify arms agreements, he wanted insurance in a dangerous world, even if Gorbachev did scale back on land-based ballistic missiles. In President Reagan's view, if practical, the SDI provided that insurance policy.

The "Qaddafis" of the Post-Soviet Period

Rogue states and substate actors, like terrorist networks, were not envisioned during the Reykjavik proceedings. And these entities now pose special dangers to the United States. Rogue nations burst on the international scene following the breakdown of the Soviet Union to preoccupy U.S. attention. The or-

9. Ibid., page 651.

igins of contemporary rogue states date from the Cold War divisions, however. Much is made, and rightly so, of the immense changes that the Soviet Union's implosion ushered into Central Europe and Central Asia. The legacy of this side of the story was freedom from Soviet rule and independent capitals, stretching from Tallinn to Tashkent. Yet, another dimension of the dissolving of Moscow's imperial apparatus has been less explored. The imploded empire left behind pernicious endowments that, like the dragon teeth sowed by the mythical Cadmus, sprang up as outlaw states. Moscow had funded, trained, and armed client states as proxies to confound the United States; they became the rogue states of the post–Berlin Wall era. North Korea and Cuba boasted avowedly Marxist-Leninist governments that masked personal authoritarianism despite Communist trappings. Other proxy states, such as Iraq, Libya, and Syria, professed a bastardized socialism through which their strongmen weaved fascistic systems, replete with secret police, subservient-party structures, and leader-praising slogans. Whatever their internal variations, these Soviet clients shared an abiding antipathy toward the West in general and the United States in particular.

History is replete with examples of rogue polities on the international scene, from the ancient Gauls to Nazi Germany, which functioned outside the world community of their eras. In the contemporary scene, rogue states demonstrate contempt for international norms by repressing their own populations, promoting international terrorism, flouting traditional diplomatic intercourse, and, most of all, seeking weapons of mass destruction (WMD). With the ouster of the Saddam Hussein regime, North Korea and Iran meet these broad criteria in spades.[10] Moreover, they cooperate with one another in developing weapons and missiles.

10. For more analysis of the rogue state phenomenon, see Thomas H. Henrik-

Both Iran and North Korea have devoted immense resources to the perfection of missiles whose range is longer and
longer as well as to secret nuclear programs with the goal of
developing atomic weapons. Iran, for example, had developed
its ballistic missile capacity in spite of setbacks. Iran's Shahab
3 medium-range missile is thought to have the capability of
reaching Saudi Arabia, Turkey, Israel, and U.S. troops sta-
tioned in the Middle East. These liquid-fueled, road-mobile
ballistic missiles are similar to the North Korean No Dong
series. The Iranian missiles are designed to carry a 1,200-
kilogram payload some 1,300 kilometers. Other longer-range
missiles, such as the Shahab 4, remain cloaked in secrecy.

In its arsenal, Tehran also has short-range, liquid-fueled
missiles of the SCUD B and SCUD C type. North Korean assistance enabled Iran to produce such projectiles on its own. The
Iranian arms inventory also includes solid-fueled missiles,
such as the Chinese-manufactured CSS-8, the type that dam-
aged an Israeli naval vessel in July.

North Korea, which is the rogue missile supply hub for il-
licit sales, is also hard at work in its research, design, and
production of advanced rocketry. The July Fourth 2006 launching of its much ballyhooed Taepodong 2 fizzled. This multi-
stage sequel was to have surpassed its progenitor, the Taepodong 1, parts of which flew 3,000 kilometers in August 1998,
when it traversed over Japan's northern islands.

Other shorter-range missiles include the SCUD-B, C, and
D variants. The SCUD-D, or No Dong, has a range of 1,000 to
1,300 kilometers, with a payload of 700 to 1,000 kilograms.
These types of weapons pose a threat to American forces
posted in South Korea and Japan.

---

sen, "The Rise and Decline of Rogue States," *Journal of International Affairs* 54,
no. 2 (Spring 2001), pages 349–373.

If the Taepodong series is perfected, then it has the potential for hitting Guam, Hawaii, Alaska's Aleutian Islands chain, perhaps even California. Neither this capability nor the miniaturization of nuclear warheads atop ballistic missiles seems to be imminently within the grasp of North Korea or Iran. But it does seem inevitable over time. The madmen that Ronald Reagan worried about are now running North Korea and Iran. Pyongyang's Kim Jong Il's regime threatens dire consequences for the United States, South Korea, or the region at any perceived provocation, and Tehran's Mahmoud Ahmadinejad harbors apocalyptic visions while he advocates wiping Israel off the map.

Along with the threats from rogue regimes, the West in general and the United States in particular face potentially catastrophic assault from terrorist networks or so-called substate entities. Groupings such as Osama bin Laden's Al Qaeda and Hassan Nasrallah's Hezbollah now complicate the international landscape as they raise difficulties for defending nation-states. It is highly unlikely that such groups will acquire sophisticated missiles for an attack against the United States; but it is not improbable beyond the realm of reason. It is more likely they would smuggle a nuclear "dirty bomb" into an American city, using regular explosives to spread nuclear materials at levels unsafe for life, thereby causing deep economic and societal disruption. But the release of toxic chemicals or deadly biological agents might do as much, or even more, harm than a nuclear "dirty bomb."[11] These threats require a set of defenses different from an anti-missile structure.

11. For information on dirty bombs, see Sidney D. Drell and James E. Goodby, *The Gravest Danger: Nuclear Weapons* (Stanford, California: Hoover Institution Press, 2003), pages 48 and 86.

Actualizing Missile Defense Plans

Unfortunately, the scenarios that the American participants at Reykjavik feared are, in fact, materializing, with the proliferation of nuclear weapons capacity and the spread of missile technology to nontransparent dictatorial regimes.

Thus the option of long-range missile defense that the United States secured at the Iceland summit stands it in much better stead than the actual progress toward an effective defensive system. Admittedly, there is as of yet no impenetrable shield. But as Reagan wrote in his autobiography, he "never viewed the SDI as an impenetrable shield—no defense could ever be expected to be 100 percent effective."[12]

Even President George W. Bush, an enthusiastic proponent of building and deploying a ground-based ballistic missile defense in Alaska and California, hedged when he expressed that he thought there was "a reasonable chance" of shooting down North Korea's Taepodong 2 this past summer if it approached American territory; its range was projected to be as far as 6,700 kilometers (4,200 miles). He added: "At least that's what the military commanders told me."[13] Even President Bush's somewhat tentative statement marked a substantial improvement from Reagan's acknowledgment that the United States lacked any defense against incoming missiles.

This is not the place to review the successes and setbacks of the various weapon systems to bat down missiles. In fact, many of these defensive efforts are not aimed at the long-range Soviet-type ICBMs that so imperiled the United States during the Cold War. Instead, they aim to "kill" the short- and medium-range missiles tested by North Korea in July. Some of

12. Reagan, *An American Life*, page 608.
13. President's White House Press Conference, July 7, 2006.

these systems, however, reach beyond Earth's atmosphere, hitting experimental targets at over 100 miles high.

Showing some promise are SM-3 interceptors from the U.S. Navy AEGIS system borne by naval destroyers and cruisers, the Army's Terminal High-Altitude Air Defense (THAAD), and the much more limited range Patriot Advanced Capability-3 system. Moreover, the United States has embarked on cooperative missile defense designs with Germany, Italy, Israel, and Japan. Partially from American support, Israel has developed its own Arrow against longer-range missiles, but not against the Katyusha and Qassam rockets that poured down on it in July and August 2006. Other countries, some long skeptical of U.S. exertions, have embarked on their own anti-missile umbrellas. For example, France is experimenting with its anti-aircraft missile, the Aster, for a defensive capability against hostile missiles.

Other experiments involving advanced laser technology, both ground- and aircraft-based concepts, are under way and hold out promise.[14] Clearly, missiles have come to stay in the world's arsenals—in nation states as well as terrorist organizations—and so have missile defenses. Still, much work remains to make a missile defense system effective, if not ever a 100-percent umbrella.[15]

Having escaped the Sirens wailing that "missile defense is not possible," the years after the Reykjavik Summit have seen the U.S. effort navigate between the Scylla of too much too soon and the Charybdis of too little too late. But like Ulysses, the current administration has sailed beyond these two mon-

14. I am grateful for Sid Drell's insights on advanced laser technology as well as on other aspects of the paper, especially on the fine points of the ABM treaty and its allowance for tactical defensive missiles.

15. Dave Ahearn, "ABL, KEI Missile Shields Must Improve: Obering," *Defense Daily* (August 17, 2006), page 1.

sters in deploying a limited defense system in hopes of avoid-
ing catastrophic consequences. It was the Reykjavik decision
that made this course possible by not trading away American
security. Had the Reykjavik negotiators traded away the SDI,
the decision might have sent a chill on all antimissile defense
experiments. Instead, work could go forward. The advances in
SDI research could thus be integrated with tactical-level systems. Thus, by holding on to the SDI, the Reagan administration at the least paved the way for President Bush to declare
that the United States had a "reasonable"—rather than no—
chance of intercepting a North Korean long-range ballistic
missile.

At this point, twenty years later, the Reykjavik decision
looks inspired as we face an ever more perilous world. One
mark of a higher order of statecraft involves the success of
preserving a nation's long-term security in the pursuit of its
short-term interests. In this realm, the legacy of Reykjavik
shines brightly.

The Soviet Preparation
for Reykjavik:
Four Documents

David Holloway

The Documents

The four documents attached to this memorandum come from
the Kataev papers, which are lodged at the Hoover Archive.
(The translations are by Natalya Porfirenko of the Hoover Institution.) At the time of the Reykjavik meeting, Vitalii Kataev
was deputy chief of the Defense Industries Department in the
apparatus of the Central Committee of the Communist Party
of the Soviet Union. An engineer by training, he had worked
in the "Yuzhnoe" missile design bureau in Dnepropetrovsk. He
joined the Central Committee staff in 1974. Besides holding the
position of deputy chief of a department, he was also head of
a special section in the Defense Industries Department dealing
with disarmament. He was thus intimately involved in the formulation and coordination of Soviet arms control policy.

Document 1, *Material on Nuclear-Space Arms in Preparation for the Meeting with R. Reagan,* is much longer than the
others. It was evidently prepared as background for the Soviet
position. The most interesting elements are perhaps the as-
sessments of the relative standing of Soviet and American R&D

David Holloway is the Raymond A. Spruance Professor of International History,
Professor of Political Science, and Senior Fellow at the Freeman Spogli Institute
of International Studies at Stanford University. He is the author of *Stalin and the
Bomb* (Yale University Press 1994).

with respect to nuclear weapons and ballistic missile defense. (Kataev Collection, Box 2.)

Document 2, *Thoughts for the meeting with R. Reagan*, draws heavily on Document 1 in the recommendations it makes. (Kataev Collection, Box 1.)

Document 3, *Central Committee of the Communist Party of the Soviet Union*, was written after Document 2. Among the signatories are: the head of the Politburo commission for overseeing negotiations and Central Committee secretary responsible for the defense industry, Lev Zaikov; the head of the KGB, Viktor Chebrikov; the defense minister, Sergei Sokolov; two Central Committee secretaries Anatolii Dobrynin and Aleksandr Yakovlev; and the first deputy minister of foreign affairs, Anatolii Kovalev. (Kataev Collection, Box 1.)

Document 4, *Key Positions*, sets out the Soviet position for Reykjavik. Attached to this document are the directives that the Soviet Union hoped would be issued by the General Secretary and the President to the Foreign Minister and the Secretary of State, if the meeting proved successful. Also attached is the draft resolution for the Politburo approving the key positions and the directives. (Kataev Collection, Box 1.)

The Context

The best way to provide the context for these documents is to look briefly at the account given of the Soviet preparation for Reykjavik by Anatolii Chernyaev, Gorbachev's foreign policy advisor.[1] The idea of the Reykjavik meeting came to Gorbachev in August, when he was on vacation in the Crimea. He was frustrated by the slow progress at the negotiations in Geneva and wanted to breathe new life into the process of arms reduction.

1. A. S. Cherniaev, *Shest' let s Gorbachevym* (Moscow: Kul'tura, 1993), pp. 105–117.

Gorbachev instructed Chernyaev to ask the Foreign Ministry to work out the specifics for a meeting with Reagan, but Chernyaev was very disappointed with the result. He told Anatolii Kovalev, first deputy foreign minister, that the most important thing was "big politics," not the details of negotiation.[2]

A few days before Gorbachev left for Reykjavik, the Politburo met to discuss draft directives that had been prepared by Marshal S. F. Akhromeev, Georgii Kornienko, and Yulii Vorontsov. On the day before the Politburo meeting, Chernyaev gave Gorbachev his own assessment of the draft by Akhromeev and his colleagues. It was not favorable. He did not think that the draft would serve Gorbachev's purpose of stunning Reagan with daring proposals. The Soviet position, he thought, should start with strategic weapons, not with nuclear tests and space. Gorbachev should repeat his commitment to eliminate nuclear weapons, and renew the proposal to cut strategic weapons by 50 percent in the first stage. Then should come medium-range systems: Gorbachev should propose elimination of all medium-range missiles in Europe and leave the British and French forces to one side. The ABM issue should not be linked, in the first instance, with the issue of reductions in strategic arms, but rather with the banning nuclear tests: "if there are no tests, there will be no SDI."[3]

At the Politburo meeting, Gorbachev rejected the Akhromeev-Kornienko-Vorontsov draft and adopted most of Chernyaev's suggestions. According to Chernyaev's notes, Gorbachev summed up the Politburo meeting as follows: "Our main goal now is to prevent another new stage in the arms race from taking place. If we do not do that, the danger for us will grow. By not retreating on some specific, even very im-

2. Ibid. p. 107.
3. Ibid. p. 111.

portant questions, from what we have stood firm on for a long time, we will lose the main thing. We will be drawn into an arms race that is beyond our strength. We will lose, because now for us that race is already at the limit of our possibilities."[4]

Some Comments

Document 1 (*Material on Nuclear and Space Weapons*) may be the initial document prepared by the Ministry of Foreign Affairs that Chernyaev was so unhappy with, but it might also have been prepared by another agency. Document 2 (*Thoughts for the Meeting*) seems, from internal evidence, to correspond to the draft instruction prepared by Akhromeev and his colleagues. It is not clear where Document 3 (*Central Committee*) fits into the policy process. It includes the proposal to eliminate all medium-range missiles in Europe, but it still leads with the nuclear testing and space issues. Chernyaev's influence on the Soviet position at Reykjavik is evident from Document 4 (*Key Positions*).

These documents show how much evolution there was in the position Gorbachev would take at Reykjavik. He and Chernyaev were deeply involved in the process of preparing that position, and they were willing and able to override important institutional interests in defining it. Nevertheless, the fact that there was a Politburo resolution approving Gorbachev's negotiating points probably means that he could not go beyond them.

SDI and the Soviet responses to it receive a good deal of

4. Ibid. pp. 112–113. These notes correspond to the minutes of the Politburo meeting given in *V Politburo TsK KPSS . . . Po zapisiam Anatoliia Cherniaeva, Vadima Medvedeva, Georgiia Shakhnazarova (1985-1991)* (Moscow: Al'pina, 2006) pp. 85–87. The minutes of the Politburo meeting in English can be found, along with other relevant documents, in *The Reykjavik File* at the National Security Archive (http://www.gwu.edu/~nsarchiv/NSAEBB/NSAEBB203/index.htm).

attention in these documents, but there is little technical criticism of the U.S. program, apart from some muted comments in Document 1. Kataev later regretted that Soviet specialists did not pay sufficient attention to the critical analyses of SDI by "several groups of American scholars at Stanford and Cornell universities, at the American Academy of Arts and Sciences, at the IBM Corporation, including S. Drell, F. Long, R. Garwin."[5]

DOCUMENT 1
Material on Nuclear-Space Arms in Preparation for the Meeting with R. Reagan

I. Ban on nuclear testing

1) Possible proposals for a bilateral moratorium on nuclear testing by the USSR & the USA.

a) Propose to the USA that it conclude an agreement on a bilateral moratorium on nuclear testing by the USSR and the USA (preferably before the end of our own moratorium) for any period of time. Moreover, immediately after the start of the moratorium begin negotiations on the total banning of nuclear tests. The longer the moratorium—the better; it will reduce the advantages attained by the USA during our unilateral moratorium.

b) If the US refuses to join the moratorium starting January 1, 1987, propose that it agree to a comprehensive ban on nuclear testing or a bilateral moratorium in one or two years.

This time interval will allow us to conduct tests, on a speeded-

5. Vitalii Kataev, "Kakoi byla reaktsiia v SSSR na zaiavleniia R. Reigana o ravertyvanii rabot v SShA po SOI," Kataev Collection, Box 7, CD — COI, p. 5.

up schedule, in accordance with our existing program of nuclear arms modernization and eliminate the lag created as a result of our unilateral moratorium, especially in the development of weapons based on new principles. The test yield threshold of 150 kilotons (kt) will be respected under this arrangement.

c) For the purpose of softening the negative reaction of world public opinion to the resumption of nuclear tests by the USSR for the aforementioned one to two years, we can offer to lower the yield threshold of our tests to a level that limits the possibility of developing strategic nuclear weapons and of creating third-generation weapons with nuclear pumping (an evaluation of the acceptable yield threshold is given below).

Over the course of negotiations several test levels could be considered.

d) For these purposes we can agree to a proposal put forth by a number of countries to set an annual quota on the number of nuclear tests conducted by the USSR and the USA, possibly in conjunction with a limit on the yield threshold.

A base-level proposal including 10 blasts a year is acceptable, including: two tests of 150kt each, four tests of 50kt each, and four tests of less than 20kt.

2) Proposals regarding yield thresholds for nuclear weapons tests

a) The accepted threshold of 150kt allows us and the Americans to develop nuclear charges for all types of arms up to 600kt, including weapons based on new principles (directed energy) which are being created for national missile defense (BMD) and Space-based Strike Systems (SSS). It is possible to create, with confidence, charges with yields 3-4 times greater than the threshold.

b) Lowering the threshold to 100kt will not in practice change anything for us or for the Americans. New nuclear charges will be created for all types of arms (the same as with 150kt threshold) and the arms race will continue with the creation of ever newer types of nuclear weapons.

c) With the threshold set at 50kt, it is possible for us and the Americans to develop nuclear charges that are one-and-a-half to two times more powerful than the threshold (around 100kt). With this yield it will be possible to develop directed energy weapons, tactical nuclear weapons and a limited range of strategic nuclear weapons (up to 100kt); sharper limitations will arise if the threshold is reduced further.

d) With a threshold of 20-30kt it is possible to develop most of the systems for BMD and SSS (X-Ray lasers, boosted & directed electromagnetic pulse, directed X-Rays, high-frequency directed energy, and kinetic energy).

The development of weapons for strategic weapons to counteract the American SDI program will be precluded, but the development of charges for tactical weapons will continue.

e) Lowering the threshold to 10kt will prevent the Americans and us from developing nuclear charges more powerful than 15kt. It will restrict the development of combat models of directed-energy weapons with the required specifications. Work to complete the development of tactical nuclear charges will continue, as will elucidation of the possibilities of creating weapons based on new principles, and theoretical calculations and experimental research on the creation of models of charges up to 100–150kt will continue, with possible tests in the future, should the threshold be raised.

f) With a threshold of 1kt it will be impossible to develop any thermonuclear charges including for weapons based on new principles. It will be possible to work on the development of kinetic weapons with limited effectiveness characteristics; to perfect the elements of equipment for generating directed electromagnetic pulse; to test arms and military equipment for their ability to withstand the effects of nuclear explosions; and to conduct theoretical calculations and experimental work to provide the scientific basis for the further development of nuclear weapons. Keeping in mind that the US has a more powerful computing and experimental base, it will possess certain advantages at this threshold.

Therefore, the most acceptable thresholds limiting the further development of nuclear weapons, but in practice not harming the other side, are in the 10–50kt range. With a reduction of the threshold yield to below 10kt, the USA will have certain advantages in further improving their nuclear weapons due to their more powerful computing and experimental base.

3) The state and time-tables of work on directed energy nuclear weapons

The main reason why the US refused to join our unilateral moratorium is their desire to complete research on the design concept for directed-energy nuclear weapons, work on which began in US in the 1970s.

The principle of action of the new type of weapons consists in transforming part of the energy from a nuclear explosion into powerful streams of directed X-rays or electromagnetic radiation or a stream of high-energy particles. Such directed streams are capable of disseminating a distance of several thousand kilometers in space, and weapons systems created on their basis are capable of striking, in space or from space, ballistic missiles, their warheads, satellites and other targets at those distances.

Moreover, work is being conducted in the US on the creation of kinetic energy nuclear weapons, in which a nuclear explosion creates a stream of metallic fragments of small mass that travel at more than ten kilometers per second and are capable of striking targets in space, including warheads, with a direct hit.

According to our sources, the Americans have conducted 10 underground nuclear tests for the purpose of creating an X-ray laser weapon. No less than three tests were conducted towards the creation of directed electro-magnetic radiation weapons, and two tests were performed in relation to kinetic energy weapons. The nuclear tests that were conducted for the purpose of creating these types of weapons took place during our moratorium.

Full-scale development of these weapons is expected to occur in the second half of the 1990s.

In the USSR, research on the possibility of creating directed energy nuclear devices analogous to those being developed in the USA has been ongoing since the late 1970s. Beginning in 1980, there have been 5 underground nuclear tests conducted in our country to study the possibility of creating nuclear-pumped X-ray lasers. Three further tests were prepared but postponed in connection with the announcement of our moratorium. One underground test was conducted to evaluate the feasibility of kinetic energy weapons; the test showed the potential plausibility of accelerating a small mass to high speeds.

Considering that the US has conducted more research on the creation of directed energy nuclear weapons, has a better experimental laboratory base, and has continued nuclear tests for this type of weapon over the period of our moratorium, the US has achieved results in this area which surpass those of our country.

With a complete ban on nuclear testing or a bilateral moratorium, full-scale development of directed energy weapons would be completely excluded both in the US and in our own country.

4) The consequences of a complete ban on nuclear weapon testing for the development of our country's strategic arms.

The technical level of the strategic nuclear forces (SNF) of the USSR is on a par with the level of strategic offensive forces of the United States. Given a complete ban on nuclear tests, the combat effectiveness of the SNF could be maintained at the current level for the next 5–10 years through the production of nuclear charges already developed and tested according to existing technology.

a) However, under these conditions it will be impossible to modernize/improve them (the charges) or raise their combat effectiveness. Development of future warheads for strategic systems such as the land-based RT-23 UTTH system, the sea-based D-19 UTTH system, and the air-launched strategic cruise missiles (Kh-90 and Kh-90S) will become more complex. Ground-penetrating nuclear munitions for striking heavily defended targets will not be created, nor will warheads with an "untouchable" regime.

b) The most negative effects of a complete ban on nuclear tests would affect our strategic defensive arms. The possibility of developing nuclear weapons of the new generation—directed energy weapons (X-ray lasers, high-intensity electromagnetic and super-high frequency radiation, kinetic, etc.) for space-based anti-missile systems will be completely excluded. X-ray warheads will not be created for the "Nariad—V" anti-space system and the A-135 Moscow ABM system.

c) Work to check the ability of arms to withstand the effects of penetrating radiation from nuclear explosions will cease, since currently only by means of nuclear explosions can one ensure the complex impact of all the factors involved in weapons effects.

Should nuclear testing cease it would be possible to confirm the combat-readiness of nuclear munitions only by calculations and modeling. However, these methods would be incomplete and will not guarantee the readiness and reliability of the munitions.

d) A unilateral cessation by the Soviet Union of nuclear testing would lead to the military-technical superiority of the United States in the area of nuclear arms, especially where the development of munitions of the new generation for strategic weapons is concerned.

In the case of a joint decision with the United States to ban nuclear tests, the existing parity will be preserved, and the possibility of developing nuclear weapons of the new generation will become problematic for both the USSR and the USA.

II. Regarding Space Weapons

1) Whose materials are being used to evaluate the condition of work on space weapons in the USSR & USA?

The development of our country's space weapons was analyzed and evaluated on the basis of directives from the Central Committee of the Communist Party and the Council of Ministers of the Soviet Union: "The main directions of development of arms and military equipment," development programs, five-year R&D plans, decisions to develop individual models and weapons systems.

The capabilities and development times of prospective space-based weapon systems are based on the reports and conclusions of governmental, inter-departmental, and expert commissions, taking account of the current state of affairs in the organizations developing the systems.

Space-based weapons of the USA are evaluated on the basis of the classified materials of the Main Intelligence Directorate (GRU) of the General Staff, the KGB, scientific-technical institutes of the Academy of Sciences and of the defense industrial ministries, as well as on open materials in the domestic and the foreign press.

Given the lack of reliable information about the opponent, it is not to be excluded that the information about certain types of weapons might be somewhat exaggerated.

The main materials used for comparing prospective space-based arms in the USSR and the USA up to the year 2000 and beyond are the conclusions of inter-departmental commissions (the commission of Academician Velikhov and others).

2) Comparative evaluation of ground-based echelons of missile defense in the USSR and the USA.

During the first stage, up to 1990, the US will continue R&D on short- and long-range interception.

The USSR will conduct similar work, and in addition the Moscow "A-135" missile defense system will enter into service.

During the second stage, up to 1995, the US could begin the testing and then the deployment of all three complexes for close, medium, and long-range interception: Sentry, HEDS, and ERIS.

The USSR plans to complete development and begin deployment of the "Sambo" complex for close interception for defense of command posts and missile silos, and the "S-550" medium range system for the defense of especially vital administrative and industrial centers.

During the third stage, up to the year 2000 the US might numerically increase the ground-based echelon.

The USSR plans to deploy the "A-235" for the defense of Moscow and the Moscow industrial region.

Overall, work on creation of the ground-based missile defense echelon in the Soviet Union and the US is at approximately the same level.

3) Comparative evaluation of the state of work on the space-based echelons of BMD in the USSR and the USA.

During the first stage, up to 1990, the US plans demonstration tests of prototypes of elements of prospective space weapons for destroying ballistic missiles. The USSR plans to conduct only fundamental and exploratory research into space-based missile defense systems.

During the second stage, up to 1995, the US plans demonstration tests of space-based kinetic and laser weapons for intercepting ICBMs in the ballistic & terminal stages of their flight trajectory. Furthermore, the US plans to work out the principles for interacting with information systems. The USSR plans to develop a demonstration-test model only with missile weapons.

During the third stage up to 2000 the US might begin deployment of a group of space-based systems with missile weapons and might continue to conduct tests in space of electro-dynamic and laser weapons.

At this stage, the USSR can conduct flight tests of space systems with laser and electro-dynamic weapons.

The full-scale deployment of space-based missile-defense systems can be expected after 2010. We need to bear this in mind while looking at our own programs.

Overall, the Soviet Union lags approximately 4–5 years behind the United States in research on creating the elements of a space-based missile defense echelon.

4) Why are we lagging behind the US in the development of a multi-echeloned Missile Defense System?

We lag for two reasons. The *first* is the poorer technological quality (compared to the US) of the basic critical elements required for multi-stage missile defense: optical-electronic systems, small high-performance computers, laser gyroscopes, cryogenic systems, etc.

The Americans are close to completing work on heat-seeking

guidance for interceptor missiles with infra-red self-guided warheads. We have not developed models of this type of technology.

Comparison of the technical characteristics of the elements being developed in the USSR and the USA shows a technological lag on the part of the USSR in the production of hyper-clean materials for receivers and integrated circuits, in the degree of integration of the elements, in the precision of diamond-polished optics, in the creation of hyper-sensitive deep-cooled receivers in the long-wave infrared spectrum, and in the creation of smaller on-board computers.

The second is the insufficient development of the test base and the limited quantity of high-performance equipment for the processing and manufacture of complex elements of space technology.

Moreover, we began work on space-based strike systems later than the United States, as a responsive measure. We have been able to devote fewer scientific and industrial resources to this area based on our existing capabilities.

5) Is it possible to create a perfect multi-echelon Missile Defense System to intercept all incoming warheads?

An evaluation of the possibilities of the SDI system currently being developed by the United States shows that 100 percent interception of all missiles and warheads is in practice impossible.

An analysis conducted by the Ministry of Defense, together with industry (Research programs: "Duel-2," "Vekha-2," "Countermeasures"), shows that around 2010–2020, even with the creation of several missile-defense echelons, the effectiveness of the US BMD System—and then only theoretically—will be approximately 99% (i.e. 1% of warheads will be able to penetrate to their intended targets).

As far as the final American goals in creating a full-scale BMD system are concerned, an analysis based on classified and unclassified materials, conducted by the Inter-departmental working group comprised of the leading specialists from industrial organizations, the Academy of Sciences and the Ministry of Defense (created by the Military-Industrial Commission on June 6, 1985), shows that the Americans think that a multi-echelon missile defense system should allow, at most, 0.1% of the attacking missiles to get through.

It will be possible to evaluate the real prospects of achieving such BMD effectiveness only after the problem of creating weapons based on new physical principles, of nuclear weapons of the third generation, is solved, and by taking account of the measures which the other side can take to overcome or destroy the multi-echelon missile defense system.

Only in the mid-1990s, if a treaty banning nuclear tests is not concluded, will there be the basis for a real assessment of the time it will take to build a national BMD system in the United States.

6) Is it possible to distinguish reliably between offensive and defensive space-based systems?

Any space-based system carrying strike weapons (kinetic, energy beam, nuclear) is both offensive and defensive.

There is no basis for separating space-based strike systems into offensive and purely defensive categories. This distinction is useful to the US to mask the true goals of creating a multi-echelon missile defense system (SDI). In reality, this is a strategic offensive system designed to destroy the warheads of our missiles and also other objects in space, on earth and in the air.

It is possible for the Soviet Union to recognize the presence of these strike systems in space. Before entering service, they will go through a phase of development and testing in space. The space-based strike group will grow gradually and be placed into orbit at various altitudes and angles. To destroy our missiles and warheads, the US will need to put into space hundreds of space strike vehicles. That is why we have created and deployed a space-monitoring system. The USA will not be able to deploy these assets without our observing them.

Our national means of inspection allow us to determine if an object in space has nuclear weapons on board. It is extremely difficult to determine by technical means the presence of other weapons.

7) Why it is necessary for the USSR to keep the 1972 ABM Treaty in effect for no less than 10 years?

Ever since it entered into force in 1972, the ABM Treaty has been considered by us to be the foundation of the system of international agreements on arms limitation and reduction. Only mutual restraint in the area of BMD makes it possible to make progress in restraining the race in strategic offensive arms. The treaty is of unlimited duration (art. XV). In that regard our position remains unchanged: to maintain the ABM Treaty regime. This is necessary for us as we seek to delay the creation by the US of a multi-echeloned missile defense system, to gain time to conduct analogous work in our own country, and to develop counter-measures against the US BMD.

For that we must gain agreement that the USA and the USSR will not withdraw from the treaty for up to 15 years and will observe all of its provisions, including the ban on deploying ABM systems for the defense of the territory of the country. It is especially important to achieve a ban on development (except for laboratory work) and testing of space-based systems and components.

It would be possible to accept an agreement not to withdraw from the treaty for 10 years on condition that all of its provisions are observed, and then, in the following five years, to conduct negotiations on the problem of national multi-echelon BMD system and strike space systems. As a last resort, the timing of the negotiations could be shortened to 2.5–3.0 years.

8) Why and for what purpose did the Soviet Union create an anti-satellite system?

The work done in the 1960s to develop a Soviet anti-satellite system was a necessary response to the creation in the U.S. of ground-based missile complexes such as "Nike-Zeus" and "Nike-Hercules." These missiles could have been used by the Americans to destroy low-orbiting Soviet national technical means of verification, and communications and navigation satellites.

In 1983 the Soviet Union unilaterally announced a moratorium on the testing of its anti-satellite system, abandoned its deployment, and ceased the launch of "IS-M" satellites.

The USSR is proposing to conclude a bilateral agreement banning the testing and deployment of anti-satellite systems.

9) Why does the Soviet Union launch 4–5 times more space vehicles than the United States?

There are in space, on a permanent basis, about 170 space vehicles operated by the Soviet Union, and about 150 by the United States.

We conduct about 100 launches per year, the United States about 20. The disparity in the number of launches (approximately 5 times), despite an almost identical number of continuously operated space vehicles in orbit, can be explained mainly by the shorter life-span of our space vehicles.

III. Strategic Offensive Weapons

1) Why is the problem of reducing strategic offensive arms connected to the ban on creating a broad-scale ABM system with space-based components?

This is not a new problem. The USSR and the USA encountered it at the end of the 1960s in the process of working out SALT-1. At that time, the USA was creating a limited ground-based ABM system (Safeguard), and even then it became apparent that if one side creates an ABM defense, then the other side is forced to search for means and methods of overcoming it, in order to prevent the opponent from destroying its offensive capabilities.

In the course of the negotiations, both sides jointly acknowledged that there is an unbreakable link between strategic offensive and defensive systems. It is not a coincidence that in 1972 the USSR and the USA simultaneously signed the ABM Treaty and the Interim SALT Agreement. Moreover, both sides indicated in the aforementioned documents that only mutual restraint in the area of missile defense would make it possible to move forward to limit and reduce strategic offensive arms.

Now the USA has decided to break that linkage. It intends to deploy a space echelon for national BMD, on the basis of weapons being developed on new physical principles. Such a BMD system, combined with the growth of strategic offensive arms, is designed to create a first-strike capability without the fear of retaliation. In other words, the aim is to disarm us in the face of the U.S. nuclear threat. Under these conditions it would be impossible for the Soviet Union to reduce its strategic nuclear forces because that would objectively help the United States to achieve a decisive military advantage over us. There will be one result: an uncontrolled arms race.

2) Under what conditions would the USSR agree to cut its strategic offensive weapons by 50%?

A radical reduction (by 50%) of strategic offensive arms would be possible under the following conditions:

First — if the USSR and the USA do not withdraw from the 1972 ABM Treaty for a period of up to 15 years and observe all of its provisions including the ban on development (except in laboratories), testing, and deployment of space-based missile-defense systems and components. It would be possible to agree not to withdraw from the ABM Treaty and to carry out its provisions for ten years, and then, in the next five years (or even 2.5-3 years), to conduct negotiations on the problem of multi-echeloned missile-defense systems and space-based strike systems.

Second — if strategic offensive arms are considered as a "package." All components (ICBMs, SLBMs, and heavy bombers) must be subject to reduction to the agreed levels in the number of delivery systems as well as warheads. Each side would retain the sovereign right to determine the numerical composition of its weapons within the framework of the maximum overall levels for strategic offensive arms. No component of the strategic offensive arms could have more than 60% of the charges in the total.

Third — long-range sea-launched cruise missiles should be

limited (the US plans on having 4,000 units) and included in the overall total for strategic offensive arms. These missiles should only be deployed on certain (agreed) types of submarines. It would be possible to include sea-launched cruise missiles in a sub-total (for example, 400 for each side) without including them in the overall framework of warheads and delivery systems of strategic offensive arms.

Fourth — mobile land-based missile complexes should be permitted, so that the survivability of our ICBM force can be maintained in the case of a sharp overall reduction of strategic offensive arms. For the purposes of verification, an appropriate system has been developed with the use of national technical means.

3) How does the Soviet Union intend to take account of sea-launched cruise missiles?

Sea-launched cruise missiles with a range of more than 600km are a new type of nuclear weapon and according to the classification of SALT II they are strategic weapons. They should be counted.

We propose to count them in one of two ways: 1) to include them in the overall strategic offensive arms framework or 2) not to include them in the overall framework, but to limit them under a separate agreed sub-level. In both cases the cruise missiles would be restricted to specific types of submarines (two types for each side).

The verification of these limitations could be achieved with the help of national technical means on both sides, and in certain cases through agreed measures, even up to on-site inspections. Furthermore, in relation to verification the Soviet side is proceeding from the following: if a cruise missile has undergone flight tests with a range of more than 600km, all cruise missiles of that type would fall under the limit; cruise missiles with a range less than 600km must be differentiated from long-range cruise missiles, otherwise they too would fall under the limit. Any cruise missiles with a range over 600km should be considered a nuclear delivery system, regardless of its actual payload, and be included under the appropriate limits on nuclear charges. Long-range cruise missiles should not be deployed on surface ships.

4) How should heavy bombers armed with nuclear weapons & SRAM missiles be counted in the totals for strategic offensive arms?

We agree that each heavy bomber equipped to carry only nuclear bombs and short-range guided missiles (type SRAM) should be counted as "1 unit" for both delivery systems and warheads.

5) At what stage of the negotiations on nuclear and space arms would it be possible to remove the question regarding U.S. forward-based nuclear weapons?

The Soviet side has never removed the question regarding forward-based American nuclear weapons/capabilities during START. These weapons supplement US strategic capabilities and represent a real threat to the territory of the Soviet Union.

If we did not push for a cardinal resolution of this question during SALT-I and SALT-II, that was only because, with a small reduction in the level of strategic armaments, the correlation of forces was not substantially affected by these forward-based systems. Now, however, when there is talk of reducing strategic offensive arms by 50%, the weight of these forward-deployed American systems grows immeasurably in importance in the overall balance of forces. Therefore, we must not let them out of our sight.

Only if the US agreed to a solution of the problem of space weapons that is acceptable to us and eliminates on a reciprocal basis their medium-range missiles in Europe, could we then not insist on complete elimination of U.S. forward-based American nuclear weapons and limit ourselves to a US commitment not to increase their number in the future.

6) Why are American proposals from 2/1/85 and 9/18/86 unacceptable to the Soviet Union?

Both US proposals are unacceptable to us for the following reasons:

First — The reduction of strategic offensive arms is being proposed without a solution of the problem of space, that is, in isolation from the ban on space-based strike weapons. We cannot do that in conditions where SDI and other strategic defensive systems are not limited.

Second — According to the American proposals, a significant part of strategic nuclear weapons would remain outside the framework of reductions: sea-launched long-range cruise-missiles (4,000 units) and SRAM missiles and atomic bombs on heavy bombers (5,000 units). This would allow the US to have roughly another 9,000 charges above the proposed limit on nuclear charges (7,500 units). This way, the quantity of nuclear warheads carried by US delivery systems would not decrease but actually increase.

Third — The suggested sub-ceilings for nuclear charges on ballistic missiles and especially ICBMs are aimed at achieving a radical break in the structure of Soviet strategic nuclear forces—on the American model. We would have to reduce sharply our heavy ICBMs, destroy the mobile ICBM launch platforms, and in their place build heavy bombers in order to observe the established limits on the components of the strategic offensive forces.

The United States would retain all of its strategic programs and would even be able to increase the warheads on its ICBMs by almost 1,000 units and reduce its strategic arms by eliminating obsolete Poseidon missiles and B-52 heavy bombers.

The purpose of these proposals is not to achieve a mutually acceptable agreement; they are aimed at giving the United States a one-sided military advantage.

7) How does the USSR propose to resolve the question of heavy ICBMs in START reductions?

The question of the Soviet SS-18 heavy ICBMs has a history of its own. It was a topic in the US-Soviet negotiations in 1974 in Vladivostok. Then it was established that the USSR had grounds for keeping the quantity of heavy missiles that it possessed at the time, as long as the question of U.S. forward-based systems remained unsolved.

The Soviet Union did not increase the quantity of its SS-18 missiles, while at the same time the US has significantly increased its forward-based nuclear systems capable of reaching the territory of the USSR. The Americans added to their arsenal the new MX ICBMs, which are just as capable as the Soviet SS-18 missiles.

	ICBM "MX" (USA)	ICBM SS-18 (USSR)
Range (km):	10,000	11,000
Accuracy (CEP), m:	130	230
Total Warheads (number x payload), kt:	10 × 600	10 × 500

Despite the facts outlined earlier, the USSR has taken into account the concerns of the United States. We are proposing deep cuts in the strategic arms of both sides, including, of course, the Soviet heavy SS-18 missiles.

8) How could verification of land-based mobile missile complexes be achieved?

Verification of mobile missile systems could be carried out by national technical means. The quantity of ground/road complexes would be verified through the number of stationary structures positioned in the deployment. Rail-based mobile systems could be tracked by the number of wagons in the train that have special distinguishing markings.

Mobile systems would be included in the totals for strategic arms once they leave the factory or other place of final assembly. These factories and assembly places would be indicated in advance, and notification would be provided of the number of complexes. Mobile complexes would be removed from the totals for strategic arms as they were being dismantled at specially designated sites known to both sides. Should it be necessary to resolve unclear cases, on-site inspections could be conducted by agreement of both sides.

9) What can be said about the division of strategic nuclear arms into "stabilizing" and "destabilizing"?

The terms "stabilizing" and "destabilizing" were introduced by the current US administration. The administration considers "destabilizing" those forces that are the most developed by the USSR and constitute its combat might—in particular the Soviet ICBMs, which, according to the Americans, should be liquidated. Those systems in which the USA is strong, such as SLBMs, "Pershing-2" missiles, and heavy bombers that can carry 20–28 cruise missiles each, are considered as forces of "stability and security."

Right now all strategic weapons are nearing each other in terms of their destructive capabilities. Between our ICBMs and the American "Trident" SLBMs there is no difference in terms of combat effectiveness (range, accuracy, and warhead yields). *This is the reason why strategic arms (ICBMs, SLBMs, and heavy bombers) should be considered together, as a united whole. This is the fundamental basis of the negotiations.* This makes possible the radical reduction of strategic arms and the drawing up of an equitable agreement that would not harm either side—on condition, of course, that space-based strike systems are banned.

10) Why is the USSR refusing to create "strategic defense" in collaboration with the USA?

If one side deploys offensive and defensive systems while the other has offensive systems, the first side attains a significant strategic advantage by acquiring the ability to launch a disarming first strike. In that case, it doesn't make any sense for the second side to reduce its strategic offensive arms. It must reserve for itself the ability to restore the strategic balance.

R. Reagan concedes this in his SDI speech on March 23rd, 1983. He states that "Defensive systems, if paired with offensive systems can be viewed as fostering an aggressive policy."

However, when *both sides* have both offensive and defensive systems, the situation becomes worse than when they have only offensive systems. Calculations show that if one side has even insignificant, minor advantages in the effectiveness of its defensive systems that immediately destabilizes the whole situation. Considering that the systems are controlled by computers, critical situations could arise. This situation remains even if there is a significant reduction in the level of offensive arms. That is, if both sides have defensive systems, reductions in the level of strategic offensive arms will not guarantee stability for either side. This is especially so if one side is clearly set on achieving superiority in defensive systems, as is the case with the United States.

Therefore, the USSR considers the simultaneous deployment of offensive and defensive systems to be inadmissible. We are for radical reductions in nuclear weapons, even for their complete elimination, but without deployment of large-scale BMD systems, without the creation of space-based strike weapons. This is the real path towards the complete liquidation of nuclear weapons.

IV. Medium-Range Missiles

1) What is the essence of the "zero-option" for reduction of medium-range missiles in the positions of the USSR & the USA?

The "zero options" of the USSR and the USA are complete opposites. The Soviet Union, in the framework of the "zero option," has proposed to eliminate all Soviet and American medium-range missiles in the *European Zone* and freeze the number of Soviet "SS-20" missiles in Eastern areas. The US would be required not to transfer its strategic and medium-range missiles to third countries, and Britain and France—not to increase their corresponding nuclear arms.

Our "zero-option" is a compromise in terms of the nuclear forces of Britain and France, making it possible to solve the problem without harming anyone's security and without upsetting the military balance.

The American "zero-option" proposes the elimination of medium-range missiles *on a global basis*. This means that the US reduces its medium-range missiles in Europe alone, while the USSR reduces its missiles both in the European part of the country and in the East. The Soviet Union is being forced to undertake unilateral disarmament, to the detriment of its own security, since the nuclear threat to the Soviet Union in the East from the US would remain the same and could even increase over time, while the Soviet means of neutralizing that threat would be subject to elimination.

The USSR is prepared to solve the question of its medium-range missiles in Asia. But at the same time the question of how to deal with American medium-range and forward-based nuclear arms deployed in the region and balanced by our medium-range SS-20 missiles, must be resolved.

Note: In the Far-East, the US has 510 medium-range and forward-deployed nuclear units/systems, including: 240 carrier-born aircraft, 124 long-range cruise missiles, 156 F-16 and F-4 jets in Japan and South Korea.

2) What is the essence of the "interim" option for reducing medium-range missiles in the positions of the USSR and the USA?

The Soviet "interim" option concerns the reduction of American and Soviet medium-range missiles in Europe down to the same level of warheads (100 warheads for each side). The USSR would then have no more than 33 SS-20 missile launchers in this region and would freeze the number of these missiles in Asia. The US could have 25 cruise missile launchers in Europe (with elimination of the Pershing-2), and on its own territory, except in Alaska, it could have a number of missiles no greater than the number of warheads on the Soviet "SS-20" missiles in Asia. The US would be obligated to not deploy its medium-range missiles in other parts of the world where they would be capable of reaching the USSR. And so, according to the interim option of arms reduction, we move towards global parity in the number of warheads on medium-range missiles, with the understanding that the USSR would keep its medium-range missiles outside of Europe, in Asia, and the US would have an adequate quantity of medium-range missiles on its own territory.

The United States proposes as its "interim" variant a reduction *on a global basis* to 200 warheads for medium-range missiles. The USSR would then have 100 warheads in Europe and in Asia. The US would have 100 warheads in Europe (including Pershing-2s) and 100 warheads on American soil, including Alaska. The American proposal is not equitable because the USSR would have to reduce its missiles several times than the United States would have to do (almost 10 times the number of missiles and warheads).

Note: The USSR in Europe and Asia has 553 medium range missiles mounted with 1363 warheads. 487 medium-range missiles and 1165 warheads would have to be reduced.

The US has 164 medium-range missiles mounted with 332 warheads. Only 33 medium-range missiles and 132 warheads would have to be dismantled (this includes the number of missiles which would have to be redeployed from Europe to the United States).

3) Why is it necessary to include the nuclear capabilities of Britain and France?

Britain and France take the view that their nuclear arms cannot present a real threat to the Soviet Union due to their insignificant number, and that they need these weapons for the purposes of national defense.

In reality, their position in NATO is different. It is NATO's Nuclear Planning Group that plans the use of British and French nuclear weapons, and in case of possible war they could be used against the Soviet Union.

With respect to the nuclear warheads of Britain and France, even now they have over 600 nuclear charges. Over the course of the next 10 years, this number is going to double. If the Soviet Union and United States were to eliminate their medium-range missiles in Europe, NATO would have a one-sided advantage. It should be borne in mind that the use of this number of weapons against the European territory of the Soviet Union, even without the use of American nuclear forces, could put the Soviet Union in a critical situation.

4) Why do we need to have 100 medium-range warheads in the West?

If our "interim" option is realized, we have to take into account the possible doubling of the nuclear forces of Britain and France over the next 10 years. This increase would put us in a situation, similar to the American "zero-option," where we would have no medium-range systems for effective retaliatory actions in a possible nuclear war.

In order to reduce somewhat the possible degree of risk, and to deter NATO countries from starting nuclear war, we are proposing an "intermediate" option which will eliminate American "Pershing-2" missiles and keep at least 100 "Pioneer" [SS-20] warheads for us.

5) Why do we need medium-range missiles in the East?

In the East, a powerful grouping has been deployed consisting of U.S. forces, the armed forces of Japan, South Korea, and other states. These forces have nuclear capabilities amounting to about 1,140 delivery systems and 2,000 warheads.

In order to fight such a powerful enemy in the conditions of nuclear war, we need to have in the East approximately as many nuclear munitions. Currently we have around 1,000 medium-range warheads, including 486 warheads on 162 "Pioneer" missiles. [PAGE CUT OFF]

DOCUMENT 2
Thoughts for the Meeting with R. Reagan

Below are some thoughts on key issues that might become the subject of discussion at the meeting with Reagan in Reykjavik with the aim of finding principled solutions to them.

1. Nuclear Tests. Maintain the principled line on a comprehensive nuclear test ban. At the same time it would be possible to accept that as a result of the meeting an agreement would be reached at least to start negotiations on this question on a bilateral or trilateral (USSR, USA, Britain) basis.

Agree that in the framework of such negotiations questions relating to the ratification of the "threshold" treaties of 1974 and 1976 will be discussed at the beginning (simultaneously express readiness to lower the threshold from 150 kt to 100 kt).

In this way, the question of ratification of the aforementioned treaties would be decided in tandem with US agreement to start completion of the comprehensive test ban treaty. In this scenario, pressure from the world community on the US for complete cessation of nuclear tests should not weaken.

2. *Space-based arms.* Besides confirming our principled line on a full ban on space-based strike arms, it would be possible to try to agree on an interim solution on the basis of a compromise taking account of both our and American proposals on the question of non-withdrawal from the ABM Treaty.

The decisive factor in defining this compromise is that for an agreed period of time, during which they will not withdraw from the Treaty, the parties will strictly abide by its terms, among them: that they will not only not deploy, but also not develop (apart from laboratory research) and will not test space-based antimissile weapons.

If the American side agrees to this well-founded formulation of the question, it would be possible to make specific in the following way our formula, contained in the letter to Reagan, about the 15-year period of non-withdrawal from the Treaty.

During the first 10 years (this would be the mean between our number "15" and the American "5") the parties would completely observe all the terms of the ABM Treaty, as was stated above.

During the subsequent period of no more than 5 years, the parties would conduct negotiations with the aim of finding further solutions in this area (if they have not succeeded in doing so before the end of the 10-year period). As a reserve position, it would be possible to reduce the period of negotiations from 5 years to 2.5–3.0 years.

Questions regarding what the parties would be permitted to do, and not permitted to do, during the period of negotiations (including the question of extra-laboratory tests of space-based ABM means and the question what to do in the event of fruitless negotiations) would be subject to further discussion, after the initial agreement is signed.

In this way, the compromise character of this option would

consist of the fact that we: 1) we accept the American framework (basic period of non-withdrawal + the period of negotiations); 2) we are reducing the basic period of non-withdrawal
from 15 to 10 years. From the American side the concession
consists in agreeing to our lawful demand that during the
agreed period of non-withdrawal from the Treaty they can not
only not deploy but also not test (outside the laboratory) anti-
missile systems and components banned by the Treaty.

If the United States does not test these weapons over the
next 10 years, that will allow us to decrease our lag behind
them in creating the space-based echelon of ABM defense. Unless they observe the requirement to ban not only deployment
but also testing, the aforementioned periods of non-withdrawal from the Treaty—whether 10 years or 15 years—will
make no real sense. A commitment by the United States only
to refrain from deploying during that period ABM elements
that are now banned would not particularly limit it, since in
any case it could not create a multi-echelon full-scale national
ABM system in that timeframe.

3. *Strategic arms.* In the event that there is an agreement
not to withdraw from the ABM Treaty, based on the compromise outlined above, then it would be possible not to oppose
setting the level for the total number of charges at 7500, as the
Americans propose, and not at 8000, as we have proposed, as
long as the same level of 1600 delivery vehicles for both sides
is established (the Americans have agreed with this figure of
ours).

It is extremely important, however, that each side should
have the right to determine for itself the composition of its own
strategic forces (ICBMs, SLBMs, and heavy bombers) within
the limits outlined above. In this connection, the United States
should withdraw its demands for establishing a sub-level of
1650 charges for heavy missiles (which for us would mean

cutting them almost by half), for reducing by 50 percent the total throw-weight of our strategic delivery vehicles, and also for banning mobile ICBMs. Acceptance of these demands would mean a radical and expensive break in the whole structure of our strategic forces, while not affecting the American structure in any way.

At the same time Reagan could be given to understand that, with a reduction in strategic delivery vehicles to 1600 and of charges to 7500, the number of our heavy missiles will in fact be reduced, though not to the extent that the United States would like (if necessary, the Ministry of Defense will report on a possible specific model of the proposed reduction in that event).

As far as long-range sea-based cruise missiles are concerned, we could agree that if they are not included in the overall number of 7,500 charges (the US will not accept their inclusion), the parties could have a certain quantity of them on specified types of submarines (the details would be subject to agreement in negotiations).

In this way, in terms of strategic arms the points on which we have moved are: 1) we agree to the number of 7500 warheads proposed by the Americans; 2) we are ready not to include in this number the sea-based cruise-missiles; 3) we indicate our willingness to reduce somewhat the number of our heavy missiles. The American side would be required to give up the manifestly unfair demands that would lead to the breaking-up of the structure of our strategic forces, which was formed as a result of objective causes, including geographic ones.

In addition, Reagan could be told that if interim agreements on space and strategic arms can be reached and implemented on the basis outlined above and if the subsequent negotiations on these questions develop in a favorable direction, then over the course of the next 10-15 years (the period of non-withdrawal from the ABM Treaty) it would be possible to reach and implement an agreement on a 50% reduction of the parties' strategic offensive aeapons.

4. *Medium-Range Missiles*. In preparing these considerations the following two options were reviewed.

First option: The USSR and the USA reduce their Medium-Range Missiles (MRMs) in Europe to the level of 100 charges on them (USSR—33 SS-20 missiles, USA—25 cruise missile launchers). The number of Soviet MRMs in the East would be frozen at the current level, and the USA could have the equivalent number of MRMs on its own territory. The number of missiles with a range less than 1000 km that the parties have would also be frozen.

In the event of such an interim option, we are willing, as we expressed for the first time in a recent letter to Reagan, to withdraw our demand that British and French nuclear weapons not be increased, and this gives us every grounds for insisting—and not without a chance of success—that in response to our great concession, the US should agree to remove all its "Pershings" from the FRG and withdraw its demand that Soviet MRM in Asia be reduced to 33 units (100 warheads), accepting a freeze at the current number.

This option is preferable for us, because, among other things, the USSR would retain 100 MRM warheads in Europe, which is extremely important for the West's understanding that we have the capability to inflict a retaliatory missile-nuclear strike against targets in Western Europe.

Second Option: Soviet and American missiles in Europe are completely eliminated, our demand that Britain and France not increase their nuclear weapons is withdrawn, and the US removes the question about Soviet missiles in Asia or that question is set aside for subsequent negotiations.

Analysis of this scenario has shown that, if with the complete elimination of our MRM from Europe we withdraw the demand that British and French nuclear weapons not grow, already by 1995 the quantitative ratio in medium-range nuclear weapons in Europe will be 2:1 in favor of NATO. What is especially dangerous is that the USSR would be left exclusively with medium-range aircraft as delivery systems (330 bombers with around 600 warheads on them), while NATO would have almost 30% of its charges on British and French Medium-Range Missiles (a total of 277 delivery systems with 1269 charges, including 1122 charges based on missiles, while we have none).

Taking this into account, it is advisable in the course of the negotiations with Reagan to try to reach an agreement based on the first (interim) option.

DOCUMENT 3
Central Committee of the Communist Party of the Soviet Union

The meeting in Reykjavik will be conducted in an atmosphere where people from all over the world, and especially in Europe, are turning towards the policies of the Soviet Union. In the United States itself people are no longer just waiting but are insisting on decisions that would stop the arms race and the descent of the world towards nuclear war.

Reagan agreed to this meeting because, due to the internal situation in the country, he can no longer, it appears, continue to maintain a negative stance on nuclear issues and US-Soviet relations. For the same reason it will be difficult for him to leave the meeting without positive results.

Thus the entire international situation is favorable to achieving a breakthrough at the meeting in Reykjavik on the main points in the field of disarmament.

From our side it is essential to take advantage of this and to propose to Reagan in Reykjavik that we reach agreement, at the level of principle, on the most important questions in the nuclear sphere. According to the results of these talks, agreed and binding directives should be given to the ministers to work out the texts of the appropriate treaties and agreements, which could be signed at the next summit meeting in Washington.

It is advisable to base the negotiations, on general as well as particular questions, not on the assumption that exchanges of nuclear strikes are possible but on the reduction of military potentials to the limits of sufficiency necessary for defense.

Taking this into account, it is possible for us to take the following position in Reykjavik:

1. *A Ban on Nuclear Weapons Tests.* We should once again firmly present to the American side the question of the necessity for a comprehensive ban on all nuclear test explosions (in that case we would evidently be required to cease peaceful nuclear explosions as well). However, our exchanges with the Americans show that this proposal remains unacceptable to them. Representatives of the current administration, including the President himself, state that unambiguously, disregarding the obvious propaganda cost to themselves. Therefore, while continuing to conduct our principled line on a cessation of nuclear tests, both in public and in our contacts with the Americans, including in Reykjavik, it would nevertheless be advisable at this stage to try to obtain from the US agreement to accept partial, but substantial, limits aimed at achieving the final objective of a complete and general ban on nuclear weapons tests.

If the American side brings up the question of ratification of the threshold treaties of 1974 and 1976, say that we are prepared to ratify these treaties and, if necessary, to make more

precise the system of verification. Emphasize that we are ready
to accept complete, effective and absolute verification. But now
the ratification of these treaties alone is no longer enough. We
need to go further. Propose, in this connection, to open negotiations on a bilateral basis, or with the participation of Britain,
on a comprehensive ban on nuclear weapons tests.

We could confirm that our moratorium will be effective
even after January 1, 1987, if the American side does not conduct nuclear explosions. It is probably not advisable for us to
accept a temporary moratorium restricted to some specific period of time.

Given that the American side is obviously not ready to
agree to a comprehensive ban on nuclear tests, it would be
advisable to propose the following option: to reduce the yield
of the explosions to 1 kiloton. If the US is not ready for this
either, we could propose that the yields of the explosions do
not exceed 5, 10, 20 or at the most 30 kt. The number of nuclear weapons tests should be limited to 2-3 per year, but not
more than four. (Note: Limiting nuclear explosions to the
threshold of 10-20 kt will cause significant difficulties for the
realization of our program in the area of space-based ABM.)

Peaceful nuclear explosions would be permitted for the in-
tensification of oil extraction, exploration of the Earth's core,
etc. Within the limits of a 20 kt yield it would be possible to
conduct 1-2 explosions a year.

The question of verification would be resolved by mutual
agreement. Here, evidently, it would be possible to agree on
any effective methods of verification, with the use of necessary
apparatus of different types. This would apply to both nuclear
weapons tests and peaceful nuclear explosions. The experience of the American scientists' use of apparatus in the region
of Semipalatinsk could be taken into account. It would be pos-

sible also not to exclude use of the American apparatus of the "Corrtex" system.

This position, which envisages concessions from both sides, would create an opportunity to pull the Americans into negotiations on the banning of nuclear tests. Such an approach could give the Americans too—if they wanted it—a way out of the general dead end in which they have put themselves by their position. We would get an opportunity to demonstrate some flexibility and at the same time to demonstrate our principled line on a comprehensive test ban, showing ourselves at the same time to be realists.

2. *Strategic offensive arms and space.* The order in which questions regarding the limitation of nuclear and space weapons will be discussed could be determined taking into account the course of the conversations with the US President.

In these questions it would be worthwhile to pay attention to the fact that the reduction of strategic offensive arms should reflect the mutual concern of both countries about the existing threat of nuclear war. That also found expression in the joint declaration on the results of the Soviet-American meeting in November of last year. It is after all the Soviet Union and the United States that have the overwhelming majority of nuclear weapons of that kind.

It would be appropriate to reaffirm our commitment to the 50% reduction in offensive arms, which was stated in the joint declaration of November 21, 1985. Of course, implementation of such reductions can take place if the parties simultaneously agree to ban space-based strike weapons, i.e. weapons which are capable of striking—from space—objects in space, in the Earth's atmosphere, and on the Earth's surface.

Say that we see, on the basis of negotiations at various levels, that the American side is interested in a different plan—an interim solution. Here an identical position on the number of delivery systems has already emerged—1,600 units each. Say also that the Soviet side is in favor of letting both sides determine, within the framework of that level, the relationship between ICBMs, SLBMs, and heavy bombers. We welcome the fact that the American side expressed at the negotiations its willingness to remove the fixed level on the number of heavy bombers that it had earlier proposed.

There is a small disagreement on the number of nuclear warheads, but this could be easily resolved. We are prepared to agree to 7,500 warheads on ICBMs, SLBMs, and heavy bombers. For ICBMs and SLBMs warheads would be calculated according to the number these missiles were tested with. For heavy bombers with cruise missiles, what would be counted is the number of cruise missiles such a bomber is equipped to carry. For a long time we disagreed about heavy bombers not equipped for cruise missiles, carrying only bombs and SRAM missiles. We think we could find a compromise here: to include these bombers in the maximum levels of delivery systems and warheads by analogy with single-warhead missiles (as one unit).

Meeting the wishes of the American side, we have expressed our readiness to set percentage limits on the number of warheads placed on specific types of strategic delivery systems -- not more than 60% of nuclear warheads on any one type of strategic delivery system, and no more than 80-85% on ICBMs and SLBMs combined. We could also make it understood that, with mutually acceptable agreements on other aspects of limiting nuclear warheads, we could accept the reduction of our heavy ICBMs to 250 units (the Americans are proposing 110-150 units).

Explain that we are prepared, taking account of the American position, not to have long-range sea-based cruise missiles included in the overall level of 7,500 warheads. The level of such missiles will be subject to agreement.

The attention of the President should be drawn to the fact that the interim option for reducing strategic offensive arms could be implemented if there is an understanding that the sides agree strictly to adhere to the ABM Treaty over an agreed sufficiently long period of time. Conduct matters so that this period should be at least 10 years. In addition, the parties would have, say, 3-5 years, for negotiations in the course of which they would decide how to proceed in regard to this question. Explain that strict observance of the ABM Treaty permits laboratory development and testing in what concerns the American SDI program and prohibits the testing of weapons created for striking from space targets in space and on the Earth. This does not entail a ban on tests of what the ABM Treaty permits. (Note: The ABM Treaty allows the testing of stationary ground-based ABM systems—anti-missiles, their launchers and radars, and also weapons based on new physical principles that are developed to replace the permitted ABM components and systems.)

3. *Medium-Range Missiles.* On this question the following possible positions can be set out. Reaffirm at the outset that the Soviet Union prefers the most radical solution to the problem of Medium-Range Missiles in Europe—the complete elimination of such missiles by the USSR and the USA while Britain and France do not increase the number of their corresponding arms, as we proposed on January 15 of this year.

As a decisive step designed to untangle the problem of Medium-Range Missiles in Europe—propose the complete elimination of American and Soviet Medium-Range Missiles in Europe, leaving to one side the nuclear arms of Britain and France. As far as Medium-Range Missiles in Asia are concerned, they would immediately become the subject of separate discussions (negotiations).

According to all data, the United States and its principal allies in NATO, in particular the Federal Republic of Germany, are clearly not prepared for such a radical solution. In these conditions we propose an "interim" solution, allowing a certain number of warheads to be left on Soviet and American Medium-Range Missiles in Europe. Recently, basically due to the efforts of the Soviet side, there have been signs that the positions of both sides have been moving closer together, along the lines of this option. At the same time a number of unresolved issues remain, and on these, it appears, will depend success in working out a mutually acceptable agreement.

In our contacts with the Americans mutual understanding has been reached that after the corresponding reductions in Europe neither the USSR nor the US would have more than 100 warheads on medium-range missiles. We argue that for the USA those should be cruise missiles, with all the "Pershing-II" missiles removed from Europe. In return we agreed not to insist on the commitment by Britain and France that they not increase their corresponding arms.

As far as Asia is concerned, the positions of the parties are still far from each other. However, here too the Soviet side is looking for possible common ground. We have already proposed to freeze our missiles in the Asian part of the USSR, having expressed our agreement at the same time that the USA can have on its territory the equivalent in warheads to our missiles. The American side has proposed to keep the number of warheads on Soviet missiles in Asia also to 100 units, with the US having the right to have the same number of warheads on its medium-range missiles on American territory. We are prepared to agree to such a solution for Asia, separate from Europe, if the United States makes the commitment to remove its Medium-Range nuclear arms from American bases in South Korea, Japan, Okinawa, and the Philippines, while simultaneously moving American aircraft carriers beyond certain boundaries.

If it is justified by the course of the negotiations, we could agree to leave a small number of "Pershing-II" missiles in Europe (no more than 18-20 units). In making the argument for just this number, one can refer to the fact that it was approximately that correlation of cruise missiles and "Pershing-IIs" that was envisaged in NATO's December 1979 decision.

Regarding missiles of shorter than medium range in Europe, deal with that question by freezing them at the current levels, say as of October 11, 1986.

Explain that a solution on Medium-Range Missiles both in Europe and separately in Asia could be reached without connection to the problems of space and of strategic arms.

4. *Chemical Weapons.* Recall that at the summit meeting in Geneva, the leaders of both countries noted the importance of solving the problem of the general and complete banning of chemical weapons. Both sides were in favor at the time of banning forever these barbaric weapons of mass destruction, and of eliminating their production base. This agreement encouraged a more active effort to draw up an international convention at the Conference on Disarmament in Geneva. Bilateral Soviet-American consultations on all aspects of banning chemical weapons have now acquired a regular basis, and this has allowed the two sides to narrow the gap on such important questions as disposing of the stockpiles of chemical weapons and eliminating the facilities for manufacturing them. In solving the question of inspections on demand we also showed sufficient flexibility by stating our willingness to seek an agreement on the basis of the British proposal, which apparently is acceptable to the United States. All this is encouraging.

At the same time there are still unresolved questions: non-production of chemical weapons in commercial industries, including private enterprises and transnational corporations; verification of all the provisions of the convention with international on-site inspections as necessary; binary chemical weapons.

Propose to the American side the following possible solutions to unresolved questions:

The USSR and USA express their readiness (and call on other states to follow suit) to have states that are party to the convention adopt the legislative, administrative, and other measures which would provide state guarantees to ensure compliance by private enterprises and transnational corporations with obligations assumed by governments; they have agreed that effective international verification, including on-site inspections, should cover both government facilities and, as necessary, private enterprises and transnational corporations, as well as their branches and subsidiaries located in other countries.

As far as binary weapons are concerned, reaffirm our position that they should be banned as representing the special danger of creating hidden military-chemical capabilities. Preparations by the United States to launch the manufacture of binary weapons do not accord with efforts to conclude the Convention quickly. The Soviet side, in directing attention to the possible negative consequences of such a step by the United States, is willing, together with representatives of the American side, to develop special effective verification measures for banning binary weapons.

If our proposals are acceptable to the American side, agree to help with concluding the Convention in Geneva in the near future, no later than the middle of 1987.

A draft of the decree is attached. Please review.

L. Zaikov, V. Chebrikov, S. Sokolov,
A. Dobrynin, A. Iakovlev, A. Kovalev

October 1986 No: _____

DOCUMENT 4

CPSU CENTRAL COMMITTEE

We present material for the negotiations of General Secretary of the CPSU Central Committee M. S. Gorbachev with President of the United States R. Reagan

1. The key positions for the talks on questions of nuclear disarmament.

2. A draft of model agreements in the form of agreed directives from the General Secretary of the CPSU Central Committee and the President of the United States to the Ministers of Foreign Affairs of the USSR and the USA on questions of nuclear disarmament.

A draft resolution of the CPSU Central Committee is attached.

We request approval.

L. Zaikov
V. Chebrikov
S. Sokolov
A. Dobrynin
A. Yakovlev
A. Kovalev

October 5, 1986

KEY POSITIONS

For the talks of General Secretary of the CPSU Central Committee M. S. Gorbachev with President of the United States of America R. Reagan on questions of nuclear disarmament

In considering the problems of nuclear disarmament, the Soviet Union starts from the position that the final result of all measures in this area ought to be the complete elimination of nuclear weapons. This has been declared by the Soviet Union and by the United States. Underline the importance of the statement of the General Secretary of the CPSU Central Committee of January 15, 1986.

Moving in this direction we ought to ensure equal security for both sides. This is the basis of our policy, and we appeal to the United States to act in the same way.

Strategic offensive arms. Both the Soviet Union and the United States have put forward a proposal to reduce strategic offensive arms by 50 percent. We confirm one more time our interest in precisely such a deep reduction and no less. All the more so since we agreed on this last year in Geneva and sealed the principle in the joint declaration of November 21. Over the last year, we have been convinced that the world is waiting, and is not only waiting but demanding that such reductions be carried out.

Insofar as strategic arms represent the foundation of the nuclear might of both sides, reductions should take place in strict compliance with the mutual interests of the sides, with constant preservation of parity, and taking account of the historical characteristics of the structure of strategic forces on each side.

We are ready to take into consideration the concerns of the United States, including those with respect to heavy missiles, and we expect the American side to show the same attention to the concerns of the Soviet Union.

Medium-range missiles. We have analyzed this problem once more in all its aspects and decided to approach it from the broadest perspective, taking into account both our own interests and the interests of our allies, as well as the interests of the United States and Western Europe.

Based on this fact, we propose the complete elimination of Soviet and American medium-range missiles in Europe. Within the framework of this decision, we are even ready, no matter how hard it is for us, to put to one side the nuclear potentials of Britain and France.

As for medium-range missiles in Asia, we propose to you, acting in the already-mentioned spirit of compromise, that the United States remove this issue, or—as a second position, that negotiations on this question take place immediately after the Soviet-American meeting in Reykjavik and be considered as an independent negotiation. As a last position—keep 100 warheads in the Asian part of the Soviet Union, and on the territory of the United States.

Simultaneously we are ready to conduct negotiations on missiles with ranges of less than 1000 kilometers.

The problems of ABM and the nuclear test ban. Confidence that the ABM Treaty will remain in force for a clearly designated period of time is the foundation on which the problems of nuclear disarmament as a whole, in the first place the reduction of strategic offensive arms, and also the cessation of nuclear tests, could find their solution.

It is precisely agreement on this account that could, like nothing else, create the trust that is so necessary for decisive steps to improve and further develop our relations.

We suggest agreeing on a compromise basis. Let us take the American approach (a basic period of non-withdrawal, plus a period negotiations) and determine jointly the period during which both sides would fully and strictly observe all the provisions of the ABM Treaty. Here it is very important to ensure mutual understanding that, along with this, development and testing in the area of SDI would be permitted within the limits of the laboratory, while at the same time tests outside the laboratory of weapons being created to strike, from space, targets in space and on the Earth would be banned. This of course would not entail a ban on tests of stationary ground systems and their components permitted by the ABM Treaty.

We propose that such a time period be quite long—10 years. Then both sides would have, let's say, 3–5 years for negotiations about how to proceed with this problem.

With regard to nuclear tests, we advocate a comprehensive and final ban on them. We propose renewing the corresponding negotiations on a bilateral or tripartite basis. During this process we agree to consider the question of such verification measures as would lead to ratification of the 1974 and 1976 "threshold" test ban treaties, with the understanding that negotiations about that would become the first stage of negotiations about a comprehensive test ban.

Start from the position that the beginning of negotiations on working out a comprehensive test ban agreement should be an indispensable condition for the process of strategic arms reduction.

Chemical weapons.   These are the same kind of inhuman weapons of mass destruction as nuclear weapons are. Their possible danger to humanity, taking improvement of the weapons into account, has not been appraised properly. We have traveled a long way in the negotiations on banning chemical weapons. We are convinced that the agreement on intensifying these efforts, which we reached last year in Geneva, has contributed to this.

Now the participants in the negotiations are close to agreement, and there are only a few questions left that need to be solved. We are ready to seek a solution to those questions on a mutually acceptable basis and in the shortest possible time.

Questions of verification.   The Soviet Union supports full and absolutely reliable verification of disarmament measures—whether in the nuclear sphere, in relation to chemical weapons or conventional armaments. We have no problem with verification. We are ready to implement verification by any means necessary, and when required—with the help of on-site inspections.

DIRECTIVES

Of the General Secretary of the CPSU Central Committee and the President of the United States of America to the Ministers of Foreign Affairs of the USSR and the United States about preparation of agreements in the area of nuclear disarmament

Having reviewed the situation on nuclear armaments and moved the positions of the two countries substantially closer during their working meeting on 11–12 October 1986 in Reykjavik (Iceland), General Secretary of the CPSU Central Committee M.S. Gorbachev and President of the United States of America R. Reagan agreed to give directives to the Ministers of Foreign Affairs of their counties to prepare for signing in Washington during the official visit of the General Secretary of the CPSU Central Committee to the United States (date of the visit . . .) the texts of agreements and accords, based on the key positions listed below:

1. *In the area of strategic arms.* An agreement to reduce by 50 percent the strategic nuclear arms of the USSR and the USA, taking into consideration the historically formed characteristics of the structure of the sides' strategic forces. With that, all types of strategic offensive weapons, including heavy missiles, will be subject to reduction within the stated frame-

work. A solution will be found also to the question of limiting
the deployment of long-range sea-based cruise missiles.

On all questions relating to the problem of strategic offensive arms, the parties will conduct negotiations with consideration for their mutual interests and concerns, displaying the
political will for an agreement.

2. *In the area of medium-range missiles.* An agreement on
the complete elimination of the medium-range missiles of the
USSR and the United States in Europe, without affecting or
taking into account the nuclear capacities of Britain and
France. Negotiations start on missiles in the parties' possession
in Europe with a range of less than 1000 kilometers.

Separately, and insofar as is practical, begin negotiations
as soon as possible about Soviet and American medium-range
missiles in Asia.

3. *On the ABM Treaty and the ban on nuclear tests.* The
USSR and the United States are reaching agreement to undertake for ten years not to exercise their existing right of withdrawal from the 1972 Treaty on the limitation of anti-ballistic
missile systems and during that period strictly to observe all
its provisions. Tests of all space-based elements of anti-missile
defense in space will be prohibited, except for research and
testing conducted in laboratories. This would not ban tests of
stationary ground systems and their components permitted by
the ABM Treaty. During the next few years the parties ought
to find, in the course of negotiations, further mutually acceptable solutions in this area.

In the shortest time that is practically possible, bilateral
(USSR and USA) negotiations on a nuclear test ban should re-
sume. In the first phase of negotiations the question of preparing for ratification the 1974 and 1976 treaties on underground nuclear explosions should be considered.

The beginning of negotiations on the question of a nuclear

test ban is a condition for working out an agreement on strategic weapons.

The General Secretary of the CPSU and the President of the United States consider that these agreements have a principled character and are a turning-point on the path to successful implementation of the tasks they laid down in Geneva in November 1985: to limit and reduce nuclear arms, to prevent an arms race in space and to end the arms race on Earth, to strengthen strategic stability and universal security.

RESOLUTION OF THE CPSU CENTRAL COMMITTEE
On the materials on questions of nuclear disarmament for the meeting of General Secretary of the CPSU Central Committee M. S. Gorbachev and President of the United States of America R. Reagan in Reykjavik on 11–12 October1986

1. Approve main positions for the talks of General Secretary of the CPSU Central Committee M.S. Gorbachev with President of the United States R. Reagan on questions of nuclear disarmament (attached).

2. Approve the draft resolutions of General Secretary of the CPSU Central Committee and President of the United States to the Ministers of Foreign Affairs of the USSR and the USA on preparation of agreements in the area of nuclear disarmament (attached).

Secretary of the Central Committee

Zero
Nuclear
Weapons

Max M. Kampelman

I CONSIDER IT A PRIVILEGE to be in your company and I know that we all consider it a privilege to have been invited here by George Shultz and Sidney Drell to note and evaluate the significance of the Reykjavik Summit twenty years ago between Ronald Reagan and Mikhail Gorbachev, both of whom agreed that "a nuclear war cannot be won and must never be fought."

It is essential, as I rise to address you, that you be aware of my reluctant view that neither of our two national political parties today has demonstrated the capacity to govern our society in this period of international crisis. I, therefore, turn to this audience of scientists and experts for guidance.

It is more than fifty-five years since I took leave from my college teaching to spend three months assisting the newly elected Senator Hubert H. Humphrey of Minnesota to organize his office—and I am still in Washington. During my teaching days, Gunnar Myrdahl published his massive study of the Negro in America. His dominant perception was the realization that wherever he went in our country, he noted a common theme—that of the principles of the Declaration of Independence. I then asked my students to recall that at the time the Declaration was adopted we had slavery, no legal equality for

Ambassador Max Kampelman was Chief U.S. Negotiator to the Conference on Security and Cooperation in Europe 1980–84 and head of the U.S. delegation to negotiate with the Soviet Union on Nuclear and Space Arms, 1985–89. He is chairman emeritus of the American Academy of Diplomacy.

women, and property qualification for voting. I could envision
the practical politician of that era saying: "This is no time for
these unrealistic dreams. We are fighting a war for our independence as a nation. Don't mix us up. We are losing the war.
Get out of our way. Slavery has been with us since the beginning of time—even the Bible tells us that."

The practical politicians of that era may have arguably
"won" the argument, but the "ought" of the Declaration has
clearly overcome the "is" of that day. The political movement
of the "is" to the "ought" has made our American democracy
the country we cherish today. The "ought" has been and is
central to our place in world history. We must not minimize
the "ought." I suggest to you that our role in the world must
be to establish a civilized "ought" for human beings—the abolition of weapons of mass destruction. The alternative is
chaos and unimaginable destruction.

In 1980, President Jimmy Carter unexpectedly asked me to
head our American delegation at a Commission on Security
and Cooperation in Europe meeting of thirty-five countries in
Madrid under the Helsinki Final Act. During the time that I
was considering the offer, a former secretary of state, a friend,
invited me to breakfast and urged me not to accept the responsibility, primarily because the Helsinki process was initiated by the Soviet Union in an effort to undermine NATO. But
I read the Helsinki agreement and found it to be an extremely
fine example of standards that should guide the human race.
This was an opportunity to move the "is" of Europe to the
agreed upon "ought." With the leadership of Shultz and Reagan, the three-year meeting totally changed the face of Europe
and contributed to the destruction of the Soviet system. Here
was a demonstration of a successful political process that
helped to move the "is" of Eastern Europe to the "ought."

In 1985, President Reagan, Secretary of State Shultz, and

Secretary of Defense Weinberger asked me to head up our negotiating team with the Soviet Union on intermediate-range nuclear forces, the Strategic Arms Reduction Talks, and missile defense. The reopening of the talks in Geneva were associated with an agreement that President Reagan and President Gorbachev would meet at a get-acquainted summit to take place in Geneva in November.

President Reagan, on his return to Washington, called a meeting of his advisors, which I attended. This was the meeting where he announced to his officials, "Maggie was right. We can do business with this man." In reporting on the substance of his talks, the president informed his staff that he had suggested to Gorbachev that it would be desirable if the negotiations could abolish nuclear weapons. It is my recollection that this news was treated with intense respectful opposition by his advisors. The president politely listened. His response to their concerns did not come until the second summit that took place in Iceland where he repeated his "zero" offer to Gorbachev and where they came close to an agreement.

Upon my return to Washington, I received a telephone call from a senior senator who asked me whether the reports were accurate on the issue of zero nuclear weapons. I said those reports were accurate, and it was clear to me the senator, a Democrat, was relieved the meeting had adjourned without an agreement.

Frankly, at that time I did not feel qualified to have a position on the issue. My instincts were with the president's objective of going to zero, but I also highly respected the fact that the experts whom I knew and worked with said that going to zero could endanger our security and that our possession of nuclear weapons was a strong deterrent against international irresponsibility.

A recent United Nations report co-authored by Bill Perry,

who is with us today, tells us that at least forty countries are today at different stages of developing their capacity to produce nuclear weapons and that more than 27,000 nuclear weapons potentially threaten our survival.

Today, I fear for the safety of my children and my grandchildren. It is this deep concern that motivates me to explore the issue and revive the Reagan objective of zero nuclear weapons. I have discussed my concerns with friends and former associates whose experience and training in this area are far more extensive than mine. Many join me in the conclusion that we must find a way to save ourselves and our children and grandchildren from the destruction that threatens us. It is this concern that presents us at this meeting with a serious challenge.

The United States and five other nations are now engaged in a diplomatic effort to convince North Korea to abandon their nuclear weapons program. The United States and a group of European nations are also in negotiations with Iran over their nuclear activities. I am not optimistic that either of these two negotiations will succeed; moreover, I fear that even if they do succeed, our success may be only temporary.

Indeed, the argument "The five permanent members of the Security Council have the bomb; India and Pakistan have it; Israel has it; what right do you have to tell us that we're of a lower grade as a nation and that we can't have it" is a powerful one. If North Korea possesses nuclear weapons, can Japan and South Korea be persuaded not to follow? If Iran develops nuclear weapons, will Turkey or Egypt or Saudi Arabia not follow?

I have concluded that the current diplomat path focusing only on the nuclear potential of North Korea and Iran is unlikely to stop either nuclear program or deal conclusively with the issues of nuclear proliferation and nuclear terrorism. If we are to give our diplomats a fighting chance and avoid the use of our military, it will be necessary to look for new means of guidance and enforcement.

It is increasingly clear to me that President Reagan was correct in urging a zero objective. What is needed today is a "Reagan-esque" initiative designed to enlarge the diplomatic canvas so that all nations can be convinced that the global elimination of nuclear weapons is in their national interest. The elimination of all nuclear arms is an "ought" that must be proclaimed and energetically pursued. It is time for us to get behind that essential "ought" and shape it into a realistic "is." We must learn from the events of September 11 that we are vulnerable—and will become increasingly vulnerable. The need for eliminating nuclear arms is today even more compelling, twenty years after Reykjavik.

It is we who must take the lead because, simply put, the United States is the world's predominant power with more deployed nuclear weapons than any other country. As the world's predominant power, it is in our national interest and our responsibility to prevent the emergence of new strategic or regional nuclear adversaries and to prevent the acquisition of a nuclear weapon by terrorists. There is today no alternative if we wish to secure the safety of our nation and of our families other than the elimination of all nuclear weapons globally, along with all other weapons of mass destruction, including biological and chemical weapons.

It is urgent that the United States exercise the global, moral, and political leadership necessary to address these related nuclear threats. It is consistent with our principles as a nation and with our modern history. In 1945, President Harry Truman joined his British and Canadian colleagues in calling for "entirely eliminating the use of atomic energy for destructive purposes." In 1952, President Dwight D. Eisenhower offered at the United Nations his Atoms for Peace proposal. As a matter of fact, the United States, Russia, Britain, France, and China are bound under the Nuclear Non-Proliferation Treaty to achieve nuclear disarmament "under strict and effective international control." Yet the United Nations tells us that there are 27,000 nuclear weapons in the world!

We cannot wish away the awful threat from nuclear weapons to the survival of the human race; but we must not resign ourselves to a nuclear disaster. We must as a nation look upon Reykjavik as a vital stepping-stone toward a rational and effective world effort to escape catastrophe and extermination.

The president of the United States, after appropriate consultation, should personally appear and propose to the United Nations that the General Assembly call for the elimination of all weapons of mass destruction. This must be our and the world's indispensable rational objective—the "ought" for the world and the human race. It should then simultaneously direct the Security Council—working with other key states, in particular, other nuclear-capable states such as Israel, India, and Pakistan—to develop effective political and technical procedures to achieve this goal, including stringent verification and severe penalties to prevent cheating by irresponsible nations and groups. Total isolation—political, economic, and cultural—must be developed to punish those criminal states that attempt to violate the "ought" adopted by the United Nations. States found to be criminal states should also lose their right to vote or participate in any way in any of the bodies within the United Nations.

In addition, all countries with weapons-grade plutonium and uranium should be required to sell their weapons-grade material to a new United Nations Bank, which would turn that dangerous material into energy available to be sold to energy-starved states in the world. It is relevant here to note that Senator Richard Lugar supports a proposal by Professor Ash Carter consistent with this objective; and just last month, the Nuclear Threat Initiative headed by former Senator Sam Nunn committed 50 million dollars toward the creation of a fuel bank administered by the IAEA.

Some may agree with the goal, but understandably question the wisdom of pursuing it at the United Nations. When President Truman went to San Francisco to address the final meeting of the United Nations Conference, he said, quite simply, that the charter of the United Nations was "a solid structure upon which we can build a better world."

Consistent with this vision, our General Assembly resolution should embrace the objective of eliminating all weapons of mass destruction globally and call on the Security Council to develop the means of doing so. We would thereby accomplish two essential objectives. First, a stamp of legitimacy by all nations would be firmly imprinted on the process and established as a goal in the minds of peoples of the world.

Second, by moving the means for action to the arena of the Security Council, we would ensure the process's taking place in a forum where the United States has, by virtue of its veto, the power to protect our interests.

To achieve the objective of a world without nuclear weapons, the Security Council will need a step-by-step process. The steps must be building blocks, not stumbling blocks; and they must be taken with urgency, not complacency. Each step should build both trust and experience that paves the way toward subsequent steps necessary for the elimination of all nuclear weapons globally, including essential verification to address the issue of cheating. One of the issues I hope we begin to come to grips with here at this conference is what these specific steps might include.

Do I expect that Russia will join us in this effort to restore sanity to the world? I do not know. Do I expect that China will refrain from exercising its veto within the Security Council and thereby try to defeat our efforts toward world sanity? I do not know.

What I do know is that an effort by us toward sanity will communicate to the world that we Americans—descendants of Russians and Chinese and Africans and Latinos and Indians and Germans and French—all of us are part of an effort to achieve human dignity and peace and that this is what America represents and seeks for all the peoples of the world. We do have the sword, but we seek a world without swords. We have the capacity to win wars, but we do not want to fight wars.

It is essential that we lead the world into developing a decisive move away from the "is"—a world with an increasing risk of catastrophe—and work toward achieving peace and stability. It was President John Kennedy who said, ". . . the world was not meant to be a prison in which man awaits his execution. . . . The weapons of war must be abolished before they abolish us." It was President Reagan who called for the abolishment of "all nuclear weapons," which he considered to be "totally irrational, totally inhumane, good for nothing but killing, possibly destructive of life on Earth and civilization."

The world knows this. It is time for us to act.

Statements by Past Presidents

President Franklin D. Roosevelt

"Truly if the genius of mankind that has invented the weapons of death cannot discover the means of preserving peace, civilization as we know it lives in an evil day."

President Harry S. Truman

"There is nothing more urgent confronting the people of all nations than the banning of all nuclear weapons under a foolproof system of international control."

President Dwight D. Eisenhower

"Let no one think that the expenditure of vast sums for weapons and systems of defense can guarantee absolute safety for the cities and citizens of any nation. The awful arithmetic of the atomic bomb does not permit any such easy solution."

President John F. Kennedy

"Every man, woman and child lives under a nuclear sword of Damocles, hanging by the slenderest of threads, capable of being cut at any moment by accident or miscalculation or by madness. The weapons of war must be abolished before they abolish us. . . . The mere existence of modern weapons . . . is a source of horror and discord and distrust."

President Lyndon B. Johnson

". . . uneasy is the peace that wears a nuclear crown. And we cannot be satisfied with a situation in which the world is capable of extinction in a moment of error, or madness, or anger."

President Richard M. Nixon

"Over 400 million people . . . would be killed in an all-out [nuclear] exchange."

President Gerald R. Ford
"The world faces an unprecedented danger in the spread of nuclear weapons technology."

President James E. Carter
"In an all-out nuclear war, more destructive power than in all of World War II would be unleashed every second during the long afternoon it would take for all the missiles and bombs to fall. A World War II every second—more people killed in the first few hours than in all the wars of history put together. The survivors, if any, would live in despair amid the poisoned ruins of a civilization that had committed suicide."

President Ronald W. Reagan
"We seek the elimination one day of nuclear weapons from the face of the earth."

President George H. W. Bush
"Schoolchildren once hid under their desks in drills to prepare for nuclear war. I saw the chance to rid our children's dreams of the nuclear nightmare, and I did."

President Bill Clinton
". . . protecting the American people from the dangers of nuclear war . . . is well worth fighting for. And I assure you, the fight is far from over."

The Legacy of Reykjavik: Outline of Remarks

Jack F. Matlock Jr.

1. THE MEETING IN REYKJAVIK was the psychological turning point in the U.S.-Soviet negotiations that subsequently ended the Cold War.

a. Mikhail Gorbachev, by early 1987, came to several important conclusions: that the Soviet Union had to end the arms race if it was to deal with its growing economic and social problems; that the reforms encouraged by the administration of Ronald Reagan were needed by the Soviet Union and in any case were necessary to end the arms race, and that he could deal with Reagan to achieve these ends.

b. Reagan was impressed by Gorbachev's apparent desire to eliminate nuclear weapons and his acceptance of the most important U.S. proposals regarding strategic and intermediate-range nuclear weapons.

c. The Reykjavik summit was the first that included extensive discussions on all four parts of the U.S. agenda: arms reduction, use of force in third countries, human rights, and building a better working relationship (euphemism for eliminating the Iron Curtain). Subsequently, this became routine and brought progress in all four areas.

Jack F. Matlock Jr. is an adjunct professor of International Relations at Columbia University, and previously Kennan Professor at the Institute for Advanced Study, Princeton. He was ambassador to the Soviet Union from 1987 to 1991. His most recent book is *Reagan and Gorbachev: How the Cold War Ended.*

d. The meeting demonstrated (eventually) both the importance and the necessity of personal communication.

2. Where we stand today.

a. Regarding nuclear weapons and nonproliferation: The momentum of destruction of nuclear weapons slowed following the Reagan and George H. W. Bush administrations. Currently reductions are without verification and do not involve destruction of the weapons.

India, Pakistan, and (by most accounts) North Korea have become nuclear weapons states, and Iran apparently has an ongoing program. Iraq was forced to abandon its program after the Gulf War, South Africa abandoned its program voluntarily, and Libya has been induced, or forced, to abandon its program. Nevertheless, it is clear that current trends will encourage more countries to try to join the nuclear club. *The mechanisms of the NPT are no longer effective and new approaches must be found.*

b. Regarding human rights: The protection of human rights improved markedly in the Soviet Union during Gorbachev's last years in office; unfortunately, these gains have not been consolidated or retained in all of the Soviet Union's successor states. Elsewhere, one can detect no overall improvement in the human rights situation. Success stories (South Africa, Cambodia) are outweighed by the tragic conditions in Sudan, Somalia, Congo, and Burma and the limitations on freedom in most Arab countries and China—to mention only a few. *We still have not found effective means to encourage the protection of human rights.*

c. Violence and terrorism: At Reykjavik, we faced a Soviet Union that still supported some forms of terrorism. That support ended, but during the 1990s, the terrorist threat to the United States increased. The United States, it turned out, was ill prepared to prevent attacks on its facilities abroad and even on its own soil. The reasons are complex, but not least was *a failure to reorient intelligence collection from traditional Cold War tasks to the infiltration and monitoring of terrorist groups.*

3. Lessons.

a. The experience of summit meetings and much more frequent meetings of foreign ministers and lower-level officials should have taught us the importance of communication and personal contact with adversaries. That importance has not always been recognized subsequently. Refusal to talk to adversary regimes has limited our ability to protect our national interest without the costly (and at times counterproductive) use of military force.

b. Reagan prepared for his summit meetings, including the one at Reykjavik, by concentrating on the psychology of the Soviet leaders—an attempt to understand their mode of thinking and to find both actions and arguments that would induce them to change their behavior. He did not assume that because Communism was bad, he could not deal effectively with the Soviet leaders. In formulating his policy, he relied primarily on those who had direct experience dealing with the Soviets rather than those who approached the Soviet Union from a distant, theoretical standpoint.

c. The three principles of "realism, strength, and dialogue," announced by Secretary of State George Shultz more than three years before Reykjavik, were the underlying principles of U.S. policy toward the Soviet Union through the Reagan and first Bush administrations. Although the United States has done pretty well in maintaining its strength since then, it has at crucial times strayed from realism and avoided dialogue. We need to put these three principles back into our diplomatic arsenal if we are to insure American security and prosperity in the future.

When Reagan and Gorbachev Reached for the Stars

Don Oberdorfer

REYKJAVIK IN MY ESTIMATION was *the* summit of the late Cold War era. All other top level Soviet meetings pale in comparison. For a host of reasons, only the Kennedy-Krushchev encounter in Vienna in 1961 can make an equal claim to historical importance. Like Reykjavik, the Vienna meeting also had unintended and unanticipated consequences—but unlike this one, the consequences in Vienna were entirely negative.

At Reykjavik in October 1986, two unconventional national leaders reached for the stars, each in his own way, but fell short at the last moment, leaving an immediate and misleading impression of dramatic failure. Eventually, however, the protagonists and their acolytes—and later, historians of the Cold War—came to realize that the summit at Hofdi House had been a great success, in some respects the greatest success in the decades-long history of arms control.

Unfortunately, I learned about Reykjavik secondhand because I was on leave as a visiting professor at Princeton that fall. It was only the Reagan-Gorbachev summit that I missed as *Washington Post* diplomatic correspondent. Immediately afterward, however, I began reconstructing the summit via in-

Don Oberdorfer covered the last decades of the Cold War as a *Washington Post* diplomatic correspondent and is the author of *The Turn: From the Cold War to a New Era* (1991), republished and updated in 1998 under the former subtitle. He is currently journalist-in-residence and chairman of the U.S.-Korea Institute at Johns Hopkins University's Paul H. Nitze School of Advanced International Studies (SAIS) in Washington, D.C.

terviews with American participants. I later augmented my knowledge with interviews with Soviet participants and access to the U.S. transcript of the meeting for my book, *The Turn*, later republished and expanded under its previous subtitle, *From the Cold War to a New Era*.[1]

Regarding the arms control consequences, it was true at Reykjavik as in all negotiations that nothing was agreed until everything was agreed. In the final moments in Reykjavik, the negotiations fell apart on the issue of the Strategic Defense Initiative (SDI). Yet all that had been put on the table by the two leaders and their arms control experts, led by the remarkable Marshal Sergei Akhromeyev on the Soviet side and the remarkable veteran Paul Nitze on the U.S. side, remained as positions that henceforth could not be denied and thus became the core of that which followed.

The Intermediate-Range Nuclear Forces (INF) Treaty, which eliminated for the first time an entire class of nuclear weapons, was a product of the deals that had been offered up at Reykjavik. Moreover, Ronald Reagan and Mikhail Gorbachev agreed in principle that over a five-year period the number of nuclear warheads would be cut by 50 percent, to 6,000 warheads on each side. It took a while and much further negotiation to validate this bargain. But a recent chart in the *Washington Post*, designed to show North Korea's nuclear standing in the international context, illustrated the current reality—5,735 operational nuclear warheads of the United States, just short of 6,000 and 5,800 operational warheads of Russia, the successor to the Soviet Union.

The arms control consequences of the summit were, in the end, historic. Ambassador Avis Bohlen, who has carefully studied arms control in the Cold War, described the principals to

---

1. Johns Hopkins University Press, 1998.

me in a recent conversation as "an odd couple on a roller coaster, each having reached the conclusion that the nuclear competition and nuclear weapons as then deployed were truly dangerous to their societies and everyone else." As Bohlen remarked, that was "a revolutionary idea."[2]

We know now that Reagan was a nuclear abolitionist. He kept telling us so in speeches to the Japanese Diet and in many other utterances, but we in the press and many in government could not square this conviction with his macho image. We didn't believe him until the news of the bargaining at Reykjavik leaked out, and we learned with surprise what had happened on Sunday afternoon, October 12, 1986.

The weight of the huge military forces and most of the political and diplomatic establishments on both sides were tugging in the opposite direction, toward more and more devastating weapons, larger and more powerful than ever before. Yet here were two men in a small room in the capital city of Iceland trying to escape the gravitational force and pull their nations back. Former Secretary of State George Shultz, on a recent trip to Reykjavik, revisited Hofdi House, now a museum. He was shocked to realize what a small room and what a tiny table had been the meeting place of Reagan and Gorbachev. From that modest launching pad they had let their hopes and dreams take flight, escaping the power of precedent and the bureaucracies—before Gorbachev brought the collaboration back to Earth with his insistence, which Reagan adamantly rejected, on curbing the SDI.

Here is an excerpt from the American "memorandum of conversation" of the last hours of the summit, as written by Thomas Simons, the U.S. note taker, and as declassified in January 2000:

2. For Bohlen's study, see Avis Bohlen, "The Rise and Fall of Arms Control," *Survival* (Autumn 2003).

The President . . . asked whether Gorbachev was saying
that beginning in the first five-year period and then going on in the second we would be reducing all nuclear
weapons—cruise missiles, battlefield weapons, sub-
launched and the like. It would be fine with him if we
eliminated all nuclear weapons.

Gorbachev said, "We can do that. We can eliminate
them."

The Secretary [Shultz] said, "Let's do it."

. . .

The President said that if they could agree to eliminate all nuclear weapons, he thought they could turn it
over to their Geneva people with that understanding,
for them to draft up that agreement, and Gorbachev
could come to the U.S. and sign it.

Gorbachev agreed.[3]

The next line, however, contained the deal-breaker: "Gorbachev continued that he now wanted to turn to the ABM
Treaty." He insisted anew that research, development, and
testing of antiballistic missile programs be confined to the laboratory. Reagan adamantly refused. After further intense argument on this point, the summit broke up.

In my view, their talk of eliminating their ballistic missiles
and their nuclear weapons within ten years was fanciful because the military and military-minded people in both countries—the conventional thinkers at home and the allies on both
sides abroad—would have rebelled at the sudden change in
direction.

I don't know what Gorbachev thought, but I can attest that

3. "Memorandum of Conversation, October 12, 1986, 3:25–6 p.m., Hofdi
House, Reykjavik," United States Department of State, Secret/Sensitive (Declassified January 14, 2000).

Reagan did not feel this way. I interviewed him for my book in Los Angeles on March 27, 1990, a little over a year after he retired from the presidency. I asked him what he believed would have happened had he and Gorbachev walked out to the steps of Hofdi House to announce an agreement to elimi-nate all the ballistic missiles or the nuclear weapons in the arsenals of the world's most militarily powerful nations.

Reagan responded that he had never considered the pos-sibility that his and Gorbachev's handiwork would have been thwarted or rejected. He might have been wrong, he said, but, he told me, with a characteristic shake of his head, "I thought the world would have greeted it with great joy."[4]

There was yet another dimension of interaction at Reyk-javik—a human dimension among leaders and diplomats—that I believe was extraordinarily important.

Here is an excerpt of the talk between Reagan and Gor-bachev as recorded in the Soviet transcript, but unaccountably absent from the U.S. transcript. It has been validated by Charles Hill, George Shultz's executive assistant and a U.S. note taker in the final afternoon. Hill recalled it vividly when I spoke to him recently. In the course of the bargaining in the decisive final afternoon was the following byplay:

Reagan. If we have eliminated all nuclear weapons, why should you be worried by the desire of one of the sides to make itself safe—just in case—from weapons which neither of us has anymore? Someone else could create missiles, and extra guarantees would be appro-priate. Your side and our side are completely eliminat-ing our weapons. I can imagine both of us in later years getting together again in Iceland to destroy the last So-

4. Interview with Ronald Reagan, March 27, 1990 (in possession of the au-thor).

viet and American missiles under triumphant circumstances. By then I'll be so old you won't even recognize
me. And you will ask in surprise, "Hey, Ron, is that really you? What are you doing here?" And we'll have a
big celebration over it.

Gorbachev. I don't know whether I'll live till that
time.

Reagan. Well, I'm certain I will.

Gorbachev. Sure you will. You've passed the dangerous age for men, and now it's smooth sailing to be a
hundred. But these dangers still lie ahead for me, for a
man they come by the age of 60 and besides, I still have
to meet with President Reagan, who I can see really
hates to give in. President Reagan wants to be the winner. But in this case, on these matters, there can be no
one winner—either we both win or we both lose. We're
in the same boat.

Reagan. I know I won't live to be a hundred if I have
to live in fear of these damned missiles.

Gorbachev. Well, let's reduce and eliminate them.[5]

Hill also alerted me to a profound change in interpersonal
relations that began for him at that meeting. He had had extensive previous experience with communist negotiators. Before Reykjavik, he told me, his Soviet interlocutors had always
stuck close to their predetermined line. "You knew you were
talking to someone doing something for some reason other
than what an individual human being would do on his own
hook. And suddenly someone at the top said, 'It's okay to be a
human being again.' And their top officials from top to bottom

5. "Transcript of Gorbachev-Reagan Reykjavik Talks: Part 4," *FBIS-USR-93-*
121, 20 September 1993. Reagan died at age 93 in June 2004.

changed. . . . Suddenly the lid was off, and you could be your-
self to a certain extent."

When I confronted members of Gorbachev's team with
Hill's quote at a Princeton University meeting of former American and Soviet negotiators in 1993, former Ambassador and
Foreign Minister Alexander Bessmertnykh responded, "For us,
of course, there were no instructions to change ourselves into
human beings, but there was something that influenced us,
and that was Gorbachev himself. . . .

"He was an absolutely new type of top leader. He was absolutely human, accessible—a man who could love, who could
curse, who could use good and unprintable language. He was
an absolutely normal man, very intellectual at the same time
and knowledgeable. In Geneva, in Reykjavik, we [Soviet and
U.S. diplomats] were getting more and more open to each
other, and this pattern of interrelationship existed for the rest
of the presidency. . . . So I would agree that one of the major
elements of changing the Cold War was changing ourselves.
We were the products of the Cold War, all of us. But we became softened by the new realities."[6]

In the aftermath of the collapse of the Soviet Union, there
is a tendency to believe that the events at Reykjavik and other
late developments in the U.S.-Soviet relationship were much
less meaningful than they seemed to be at the time—that the
Soviet Union was doomed to go down due to internal contra-
dictions and weaknesses and needed only a nudge to make it
happen.

As a historian of the period, I do not believe that is true.
Nowhere was it written in the stars that the heavily armed
Soviet Union would pass away peacefully and that the atten-

---

6. William C. Wohlforth, editor, *Witnesses to the End of the Cold War* (Balti-
more: Johns Hopkins University Press, 1996), p. 184.

dant Soviet empire in Eastern Europe and Central Asia would
pass into history with hardly a shot being fired.

It is a marvel of history that the end of Soviet power came
peacefully, bringing about the end of the Cold War. In part,
this was due to relationships that were forged at Reykjavik and
that survived the seeming failure of that summit meeting and
thrived in the months and years that followed. With different
decisions and different people, it could all have turned out very
differently for the United States and the Soviet Union, indeed,
for all humankind.

The Legacy
of Reykjavik:
Remarks

Rozanne L. Ridgway

WHEN I RECEIVED the invitation from Secretary George Shultz and Dr. Sidney Drell to participate in this conference, enclosing a preliminary program, I was delighted to accept and to pick up their offer to comment on the program as it was being developed. As you would expect, my comment was that Reykjavik was about much more than arms control and nuclear weapons reductions. Standing alone, it was but a couple of days in one small town, ending—as had so many other meetings—in the absence of agreement between the United States and the Soviet Union. However, Reykjavik, for all its importance in hindsight in the arms control arena, was of far larger significance. It was, in fact, the center point in the Cold War end game.

So this is my personal perspective—a few points that stood out in my mind as I thought about this conference.

The conduct of that end game, which probably began in the early 1980s, included a U.S./Soviet dialogue that differed in dramatic and telling ways from that of preceding decades. To be sure, we may well not have arrived at Reykjavik without

Ambassador Rozanne Ridgway is Chairman of the Board of the Baltic-American Enterprise Fund and a director of several American corporations. Her thirty-two-year career in the U.S. Foreign Service included a period as Assistant Secretary of State for Europe and Canada, in which capacity she oversaw preparations for and participated in all five Reagan-Gorbachev summits, including Reykjavik.

the strengthening of the NATO alliance and the steadfastness of our allies throughout those decades and, in some respects, without their insistence that defense be accompanied by dialogue. Dialogue in that phrase was "dialogue with the Soviet Union," but equally important was the willingness of the United States to engage in meaningful dialogue, to engage in consultations with its allies. In the case of both the Geneva and the Reykjavik meetings—there was, you will recall, a reluctance to call them summits—this meant consultations before, during, and after the event.

That said, let me take up the several elements that made up those different and telling ways that constituted the policy and process framework of the Reykjavik meeting, the agenda, and the atmosphere. If there were time, it would be informative to take up the Geneva meeting as well, but I will touch upon that historic moment only in reference to Reykjavik.

A few years before Reykjavik, and in time for Geneva, the United States had shaped the totality of its interests in the relationship with the Soviet Union into a four-point agenda: human rights, arms control, regional issues, and bilateral concerns.

Human rights issues encompassed, as examples, the treatment of dissidents (most famously Anatoly Scharansky, Andrei Sakharov, Yuri Orlov), religious freedom, travel, family reunification, denial of emigration for Jews and others, and the suppression of information. Whenever we met with Soviet leadership, the human rights discussion always began the meetings. The opening fireside chat in Geneva—President Ronald Reagan, General Secretary Mikhail Gorbachev, and two interpreters—was about human rights, emigration, and open societies. Reykjavik was no different. The meeting began with human rights.

I needn't lay out for this audience the several arms control issues except to add the footnote that there were, in the background of the more prominent nuclear matters, questions relating to conventional forces in Europe. Indeed, it was in the context of the Conference on Disarmament in Europe in the mid-1980s, dealing with transparency and conventional forces, that the Soviet Union had agreed to onsite inspections. The question of whether such inspections would be accepted was fundamentally answered by the time of Reykjavik, although some on the U.S. side had been surprised that the Soviets expected onsite inspection to be reciprocal.

Regional issues reflected the headlines of those times—Afghanistan, Nicaragua, the Middle East, Ethiopia, Cambodia, Angola—and the overall topic of Soviet support for so-called national liberation fronts. Europe was not excluded, and at the opening of the Vienna Review Conference of the Helsinki Final Act, Secretary Shultz spoke of a "Europe whole, free, and secure."

And finally came the bilateral category—trade, air safety, search and rescue, the environment, housing, consulates, and cultural exchanges.

In pursuing these interests, the United States had decided to forego "linkage" among them. Lack of progress on one would not mean the sacrifice of all others. KAL-007 did not mean we would break off intermediate-range nuclear forces and Strategic Arms Reduction Talks, terminate negotiations on a grain agreement, or cancel meetings with Soviet representatives. We would, instead, continue to press the totality of our agenda, especially human rights.

Turning away from linkage was key to moving the relationship forward, but it invited—even more than what had become normal—the predictable protests of those who saw no value in negotiations with the Soviet Union on any topic. And on the road to Reykjavik, as on the road to Geneva, there were more than enough opportunities for linking Soviet behavior to some or all of the agenda topics.

There were tragedies: Major Arthur Nicholson.

There was human drama: seaman Miroslav Medved jumping ship in New Orleans.

And there were very real diplomatic dilemmas: journalist Nick Daniloff's arrest and imprisonment in Moscow

. . . to throw everything off track.

Each was handled in its own context. Spies, an overstaffed U.N. mission, brazen electronic intrusions into the architecture of a new embassy in Moscow—they all offered opportunities to try to stop the dialogue, and when they didn't, there was always, as Secretary Shultz noted in his memoir of this period, the charge of "slave labor."

President Reagan and General Secretary Gorbachev, in the Joint Statement signed in Geneva, agreed to two summit meetings, Washington and Moscow. But Gorbachev had not budged President Reagan from the SDI in Geneva and a post-Geneva campaign to frighten the Allies had not succeeded. Elaborate personal messages with ever more elaborate arms control proposals did not move the two sides any closer to an agreement that could be the required centerpiece of a Washington summit. For the Soviets, SDI would not go away. Our best efforts at gaining their understanding of a transition from offense to defense were gaining traction at the expert level, but not at the political level. The relationship was stalled and threatened by the Daniloff affair. The Soviets, for whom the four-part agenda was at that time largely an American diplomatic fiction, took steps to undo the Daniloff knot, meet our concomitant demands for release of dissidents and intending emigrants, and prepare a summit meeting. For the Soviet Union, Reykjavik, as with Geneva, was about the SDI.

If you recall the coverage of the event, the media, the talking heads, retired generals, and diplomats saw Reykjavik as an arms control summit, the United States as unprepared for the moment, and the President as dangerously uninformed and gullible.

I would simply say that in the conversations between President Reagan and General Secretary Gorbachev, in the simultaneous negotiations being led by Paul Nitze, and my own work on all other topics, that simply was not true. We were extraordinarily well prepared. The books and proposals and issues prepared for Secretary Shultz's meetings with Andrei Gromyko, Eduard Shevardnadze, and Gorbachev in all the months before Reykjavik and Geneva, and all the work done to back up President Reagan's correspondence with Yuri Andropov and Konstantin Chernenko and Gorbachev—all of that work went with us to Reykjavik, as did our Geneva arms control negotiating teams. We were fully prepared to discuss all the regional issues and the bilateral topics. We were ready to move in any and all directions and had a delegation that could back our preparedness.

And in the human rights corner of Hofdi House, we made progress. In his day, Gromyko had declined to discuss human rights. At the Geneva Summit, it was considered a U.S. agenda item to which the Soviets objected, as always, as "interference in internal affairs," although Gorbachev and the team listened. The agreed Geneva Joint Statement refers only to humanitarian matters, which was as far as the Soviets would go, insisting that, among other reasons, the Russian language could not accommodate the precise words "human rights." At Reykjavik, the Soviet side seemed to have altered its thinking on the topic. They discovered the words "human rights" *did* translate into Russian. They signed on. Human rights *and* humanitarian affairs could be on the agenda. Where once lists and letters had to be left on the table because the Soviet side would not accept them across the table, in Reykjavik they accepted a box-load of names of intending Jewish emigrants. They were prepared to engage in discussion in which, they said, they would cite their views of our human rights transgressions. We said, "Cite away—let's discuss and agree to record our agreement to discuss again." As the Reagan-Gorbachev dialogue broke off and delegations departed Hofdi House in the instant, our progress was never recorded formally.

Some would say, and I understand this, that it wasn't much progress anyway, and others that the failure to reach recorded closure on human rights was a loss of secondary importance. However, the human rights dialogue had expanded far beyond lists of names, to discussions of open societies as successful societies, of the freedom of thought and intellectual exchange necessary to keep pace with a rapidly changing world. A far more textured and philosophical exchange was taking place under those two important words "human rights." And if self-interest weren't enough to overcome the entrenched resistance to the topic, then it helped that Max Kampelman had pointed out to them—persuasively, I believe—that the Soviet Union had signed the Helsinki Accords and, in a sovereign act, had itself agreed to the legitimacy of the topic. So where was the "interference in internal affairs"? Reykjavik probably will always be an arms control event, but it was equally important for human rights.

I've been asked to confine my remarks to fifteen minutes, and I'm sure I've passed that limit. But I would like to make one final point regarding the relevance of the Reykjavik meeting, in all its aspects, for today's nuclear challenges.

The internal burdens on the conduct of a nearly four-year dialogue by President Reagan and Secretary Shultz with the Soviet Union were enormous. There was a persistent and often debilitating effort to prevent contact, to remove substance from dialogue, to march in place or to block movement, to label those working on behalf of the president as everything from "wimps" to "symps," to misrepresent intentions, to defeat presidential decisions. I recall all too vividly that when the United States offered medical help to the Soviet Union after Chernobyl, a department that shall go unnamed refused licenses for the isotopes and machinery that make up modern nuclear medicine that were destined for Chernobyl victims. At Reykjavik, when a break in the meeting lasted longer than Gorbachev expected, President Reagan referred to his "battling bureaucracies." And there were bureaucracies on both sides tugging at coattails—or worse. One simply had to have a firm grasp on the objective and not lose heart or courage.

As well, by Reykjavik, through the care taken in Geneva to provide the right setting, to bring simultaneous translation to the summit level, and to demonstrate that social courtesies and a respectful demeanor are not signs of weakness or a willingness to sign anything, it was possible to proceed with startling candor and frankness, occasional sarcasm, and frankly aggressive diplomacy without risking irreparable harm to the interests of the United States and its allies.

Solid preparation and assembling a team of willing players are obvious ingredients for successful negotiations, but *never underestimate the power of courtesies, a fireplace, and leaders who understand the moment and are willing to grasp it.* President Reagan and General Secretary Gorbachev, however different their reasons, were such leaders.

And the rest really is history.

A Legacy
of Reykjavik:
Negotiating
with Enemies

Abraham D. Sofaer

THE EXTRAORDINARY MEETING between the United States and
the Soviet Union at Reykjavik exactly twenty years ago provided many lessons in arms control and diplomacy. Not all the
circumstances with which President Ronald Reagan and General Secretary Mikhail Gorbachev dealt continue to be relevant. Some opportunities were lost forever. But among the lessons that are of continuing value is the determination of both
leaders to engage each other despite the differences between
their countries and the manner in which each dealt with the
challenge of negotiating with a state that was his country's
main competitor if not outright enemy.

The United States currently refuses to deal, or has condi-
tioned or drastically limited its dealings, with states it regards
as irresponsible or potential enemies. At least two of those
states—Iran and North Korea—are behaving in ways that
gravely threaten international peace and security due to their
possible development and use of nuclear weapons. Other
states with which the United States has severely restricted dip-

Abraham D. Sofaer is the George P. Shultz Distinguished Scholar and Senior Fellow at the Hoover Institution, and a Courtesy Professor at Stanford Law School.
He served as a judge, and was legal adviser to the U.S. Department of State from
1985 to 1990.

lomatic negotiations are also engaged in activities that
threaten U.S. interests.

It is worthwhile, therefore, to ask how President Reagan
and Secretary Gorbachev managed to get to Reykjavik and beyond, despite the serious differences between their governments, reflected by direct and indirect hostility in several
places, active programs of espionage, economic sanctions, and
political ideologies that called for the destruction of each
other's influence and power. We should then consider how
their approach differs from the policies applied by the United
States in curtailing diplomatic engagement with its current political enemies.

The Prerequisites of U.S./Soviet Engagement

The meeting at Reykjavik did not develop out of thin air. It was
preceded by four years of conflict among Reagan's advisers
over how the U.S. government should deal with the Soviet Union. All of Reagan's principal aides shared his view that the
Soviet Union was, as he famously put it, an "evil empire" based
on oppression and actively attempting to spread socialism and
overthrow democracies through terrorism and illegal interventions.[1] All supported his vision that the Soviet system
should be consigned to the ash heap of human history. And all
supported the Reagan doctrine that asserted the right to respond reciprocally to Soviet measures based on the Brezhnev
doctrine by arming and assisting governments and political
groups the Soviets tried to undermine or oppress.

The major difference among Reagan's advisers was
whether, during this ongoing effort and as part of it, the administration should engage the Soviets diplomatically. Those

1. George P. Shultz, *Turmoil and Triumph* (New York: Macmillan, 1993), pp.
266–67. He used the phrase in a speech to the National Association of Evangelicals,
in Orlando, Florida, on March 8, 1983.

who opposed engagement with the Soviets saw it as a continuation of the policy of détente under Richard Nixon, Gerald
Ford, and Jimmy Carter, which sought a world in which the
Americans and the Soviets treated each other as equals, min-
imized hostility, and maximized stability in their relations. As
implemented, however, especially under Carter, this policy
meant a decline in U.S. influence and a growth in Soviet aggression, most dramatically evidenced by the invasion of Afghanistan. It also meant downplaying American values to
avoid offending the Soviets, as in Carter's failure to invite Alexander Solzhenitsyn to the White House. Many Reagan advisers believed that the Soviets had exploited détente to expand
their influence and power, and that confrontation, not negotiation, was the best policy for weakening the Soviets and
bringing about an end to that regime. They felt, in fact, that
negotiation was most likely to give the Soviets advantages with
little, if any, benefit to the United States and the free world.
Soviet diplomacy was built on an ideology that viewed international law as a fraudulent, capitalist system that should be
exploited through cheating and manipulation. U.S. and other
Western diplomats—ever eager to make agreements—were
also therefore a danger because they could not be trusted to
realize that the benefits of any bargain with the Soviets depended on performance, which would not be forthcoming.

Those who supported engagement with the Soviets, led by
Secretary of State George Shultz, believed that although the
United States should persist in confronting the Soviets on every
aspect of their improper behavior, the president should test the
possibility that the Soviets might be prepared to respond on
issues of interest to the United States. They wanted to see if
the pressures on the Soviets that they supported were having
an impact that could be exploited. President Reagan eventually
backed Shultz's approach. He had from his first inaugural ad-

dress promised to negotiate for peace ("We'll negotiate for it, sacrifice for it"), and he began to do so after rebuilding U.S. defenses and confronting Soviet aggression. That the Soviets cheated and lied was a given to Reagan and Shultz; but they were confident in their capacity to insist on agreements that served U.S. interests and could be verified.

This dual-track policy of pressure and persuasion differed from a full-fledged policy of détente. But it did require the administration to function on the basis of three fundamental principles that were anathema to many Cold Warriors: concepts I refer to here as *regime acceptance, limited linkage,* and *rhetorical restraint.*

The notion of *regime acceptance* meant to those seeking engagement that the United States would make no effort to overthrow or undermine the Soviet system through an attack or by providing material support to groups seeking such ends. Acceptance also implied that the U.S. government would seek to improve relations with the Soviet regime regardless of their differences. No one in any position of influence in the administration supported active efforts to overthrow the Soviet Union. But many opposed regime acceptance insofar as it could lead to accommodation or détente. They did not want to expand relations with the Soviets or to encourage cultural exchange or increased diplomatic and citizen relations. They preferred a policy of containment, keeping the Soviet Union at bay until it was unable to continue to compete. Secretary Shultz, on the other hand, convinced President Reagan to move beyond both containment and détente. He sought to focus and advance U.S. objectives by increasing diplomatic contacts at all levels, cultural and commercial contacts, and diplomatic engagement on the full range of issues. He believed these measures of acceptance would lead to increased diplomatic effectiveness if and when the Soviets were ready to move on issues of U.S. concern.

The policy of *limited linkage* was the most controversial of the changes in diplomatic policy adopted by President Reagan to enable his administration to engage the Soviets effectively. The Soviets regularly provided reasons for the United States to cite as a basis for refusing to negotiate arms reductions or anything else the Soviets wanted to achieve. Several of Reagan's principal advisers and many National Security Council specialists cited (among other things) Soviet human rights violations, foreign interventions, espionage activities, support for terrorism, and occasional acts of brutality, such as the shootdown of the Korean civilian airliner, as conduct the United States should insist must be stopped before agreeing to engage the Soviets on issues they were prepared to discuss. Secretary Shultz realized that this policy effectively prevented the United States from engaging the Soviets on issues it wished to address. He went public with the idea of limiting linkage on June 15, 1983, in testimony to the Senate Foreign Relations Committee, drafted with Jack Matlock's substantial involvement and delivered with President Reagan's approval. Shultz agreed with the Soviet skeptics that neither détente nor increased diplomatic engagement would improve Soviet behavior. He anticipated that the Soviets would behave badly in one area or another regardless of progress in the overall relationship or on specific issues. But he felt that improper Soviet conduct in each area of its activities must be met with U.S. opposition and pressure in those specific areas and not through a refusal to engage on all other issues, including those on which the United States itself wanted to engage. "Linkage," he concluded, "was inhibiting our disposition to move forcefully and, ironically, often seemed to be turned on its head by the Soviets . . . to threaten that the relationship would suffer if we undertook some action that they opposed."[2]

The notion of *rhetorical restraint* was less a matter of principle than of practice. The Soviets had come to expect (as we had) a continuing stream of political rhetoric criticizing their actions and claiming credit for every step the Soviets took that was consistent with U.S. aims. As a result, the Soviet leadership paid a price domestically and internationally every time U.S. officials claimed credit for a Soviet move in a direction the United States had advocated. Some Reagan administration officials saw this result as highly desirable because all Soviet leaders were by definition illegitimate, because none of them deserved credit for changing policies that should not have been adopted to begin with, and because the less stability such leaders had, the more likely the entire regime would be undermined.

Reagan is not remembered for restrained rhetoric. But very early on, he realized, along with Shultz, that embarrassing Soviet leaders when they responded positively to U.S. initiatives did not work. So, in urging Ambassador Anatolii Dobrynin at a private meeting on February 15, 1983, to be more responsive on human rights issues and in particular to help resolve the problem of the Pentecostals, some of whom had taken refuge in the U.S. Embassy in Moscow, President Reagan promised that if something positive were done, the United States would not "crow." The Soviets responded positively to the promise of rhetorical restraint on such issues. Dobrynin told Shultz after his meeting with Reagan that the "special subject" of the Pentecostals should be handled "privately," and the governments managed to bring an end to the issue by July of that year.[3]

2. Ibid., p. 278.
3. Ibid., pp.169–171.

President Reagan concluded it was more important to make progress on issues of concern to the United States than to make points at the expense of political opponents prepared to take the risk of compromise and accommodation.

The Reagan administration policy of confronting the Soviets, not any negotiating techniques, created the incentive for the Soviets to negotiate arms reductions. But effective diplomacy, conducted consistently with the principles of regime acceptance, limited linkage, and rhetorical restraint, made negotiations possible on a broader range of issues than would have otherwise been possible and with higher prospects of success. The increased trust that Gorbachev and Andrei Shevardnadze developed for Reagan and Shultz was based not on any belief that the U.S. administration had gone soft on its principles or objectives, but on confidence that no effort would be made to challenge the legal legitimacy of the Soviet regime, that both sides would avoid linking their many differences, and that Soviet leaders would not be publicly embarrassed when they took actions favored by the United States. Adherence to the combination of confrontation and effective diplomacy led, by October 1986, to the meeting at Reykjavik that enabled the leaders of both powers to discuss the most critical issues facing mankind in a direct, informal setting.

Diplomacy and the Reykjavik Record

The negotiating record at Reykjavik establishes that President Reagan was able to resist accepting an agreement with some results he very much wanted as the price for what he believed effective security required. He wanted to eliminate nuclear weapons through disarmament, insisting that the doctrine of mutual assured destruction was immoral. He believed that missile defense made the elimination of nuclear weapons possible by giving states the ability to defend against cheaters and madmen who might violate an agreed ban, and offered to share U.S. missile defense technology so that no state would have the advantage of such methods. By the end of the meeting, Reagan and Gorbachev had agreed on all the main issues and to the general objective of abolishing all nuclear weapons within ten years. But Gorbachev insisted on a package deal, in which the reductions would be agreed only if during that period the United States limited its antiballistic missile activities to laboratory research. Reagan refused to accept this deal despite his keen desire to reduce and eventually eliminate nuclear weapons.

The negotiating record at Reykjavik also makes clear how Reagan, and Gorbachev, adhered to and applied the three negotiating principles of regime acceptance, limited linkage, and rhetorical restraint. This is important to observe, not merely to confirm their commitment to these principles that enabled them to reach so pivotal a negotiation, but also to see that these concepts had important limits.

The premise of regime acceptance was evident at Reykjavik in several ways. As a matter of general tone, the notion of sovereign equality often surfaced. President Reagan, for example, described the meeting's objectives as being shared equally: "Both the U.S. and U.S.S.R. would like to see a world without nuclear missiles,"[4] and the Soviets insisted at several points on "equality and equal security."[5] The notion of equal or reciprocal treatment is an inevitable aspect of sovereign negotiations, and regime acceptance requires a willingness to entertain and deal seriously with such claims.

4. Memorandum of Conversation, 10:40 am–12:30 pm, Oct. 11, 1986, p. 2 (U.S. Dept. of State).

5. Ibid., p. 4. Gorbachev used this phrase in stating that "the Soviet side was in favor of proposals which were aimed at total elimination of nuclear arms, and on the way to this goal there should be equality and equal security for the Soviet Union and the United States. Any other approach would not be acceptable."

The most explicit exchange reflecting both acceptance and limitations of the concept of regime acceptance took place on October 12, 1986, after discussions had created a high degree of frustration on both sides over defensive systems and testing. When Secretary Gorbachev argued for restrictions on missile defense in order to prevent evasion, the president said Gorbachev's remarks reflected a belief that the United States was in some way trying to attain an advantage out of hostility toward the Soviet Union. He assured Gorbachev that we harbored no hostile intentions toward the Soviets. We recognized the differences in our two systems. But . . . we could live as friendly competitors.

Reagan's acceptance of the Soviet regime did not, however, mean that he would accept the notion that the United States was no less trustworthy than the Soviet Union. "Each side mistrusted the other," he said, but with regard to trustworthiness "the evidence was all on our side." In fact, the president continued, Marx (and thereafter Lenin) "expressed the view that socialism had to be global in scope to succeed," and "every Soviet leader but Gorbachev—at least so far—has endorsed in speeches to Soviet Communist Party congresses the objective of establishing a world communist state."[6] He reminded Gorbachev that when the United States had been the sole nuclear weapons power after World War II, it had offered to eliminate all such weapons, but the Soviets had refused. All of which went to prove, he asserted, that Soviet "behavior reveals a belief on the Soviets' part in a worldwide mission which gives us legitimate grounds to suspect Soviet motives," while "the Soviets had no grounds for believing that the United States wanted war."[7]

6. MOC, 10:00 am–1:35 pm, Oct. 12, 1986, p. 13.
7. Ibid., pp. 13–14.

Gorbachev did not flinch at this assault and, in fact, opened with a warning premised on his distrust of the United States. "History is full of examples of those who have sought to overcome their [Marx's and Lenin's] philosophy by force," he said. "All have failed." He advised the president "not to waste time and energy to such an end." Like Reagan, he, too, felt free, despite acceptance of the U.S. regime, to vigorously criticize the U.S. system and Reagan's own ideology. Treating Reagan's remarks as an "invitation," Gorbachev felt "obliged to say that the Soviet Union recognizes the right of the U.S. people to their own values, beliefs, society," and the right "to conduct their affairs as they see fit." He said he was surprised, therefore, to learn that President Reagan had recently reaffirmed his belief that the Soviet Union was an "evil empire," which he had originally announced with a call for "a crusade against socialism in order to relegate it to the ash heap of history."

"What would the outcome be," Gorbachev asked, "if the United States sought to act according to these principles? Would we fight one another?"

Reagan made no effort to deny holding these views, but simply reminded Gorbachev that while the United States allows free debate, including a Communist Party, only one party existed in the Soviet Union, and the Soviets "enforced rather than persuaded." A "fundamental difference" existed between the two societies, said Reagan, in that "the United States believes that people should have the right to determine their own form of government."[8] Gorbachev, no doubt eager to get back to the issues, repeated the basic principle that regardless of the fundamental differences that existed between them, each society had the right to organize itself as it saw fit, and their leaders should be able to work together as people. The Memorandum of Conversation summarized this issue as follows:

8. Ibid., p. 14.

[T]he President's remarks showed that they differed fundamentally in their basic conceptions of the world. But the two leaders seemed to agree that each side had the right to organize its society according to its own philosophical or religious beliefs. This was an issue which the two might come back to at another time. Gorbachev had no desire to quarrel. He was convinced, (in fact, that, while he and the President might have different characters and conceptions, a man-to-man relationship between them was possible.[9]

This makes clear that Reagan was willing to accept the Soviet Union as a sovereign state entitled to its form of government and that he hoped to negotiate constructively and on an equal basis with its leaders. Like Gorbachev, he stressed the fact that the individuals in power mattered and could change the world through lasting agreements.[10] He had said in December 1985, after meeting Gorbachev in Geneva, that he agreed with Margaret Thatcher's statement, "We can do business with this man."[11] But Reagan did not regard the principle of regime acceptance as precluding him from stating his view that the Soviet Union lacked political and moral legitimacy compared with the free and rational society that existed in the United States. Reagan was similarly dismissive when Gorbachev later attempted to equate aspects of the two soci-

9. Ibid., p. 15.

10. For example, he appealed to Gorbachev personally at several points, especially in urging him to accept a shared missile defense system: "He asked Gorbachev to think about us two standing there and telling the world that we have this thing, and asking others to join us in getting rid of these terrible systems." MOC, 3:30–5:40 pm, Oct. 11, 1986, p. 13. Gorbachev appealed to Reagan on a personal basis as well, telling him he would be a "great president" if he were to agree to Gorbachev's demand related to defensive systems. MOC, 3:25–6:00 pm, Oct. 12, 1986, p. 12.

11. Max Kampelman, "Bombs Away," Op-ed, *New York Times* (April 24, 2006).

eties in various ways, claiming, for example, that the Soviets would stop jamming the Voice of America if given the ability to broadcast to Americans.[12] Gorbachev was annoyed by Reagan's insistence that the United States was more humane and free—and therefore superior—to the Soviet system. But it was enough for him that Reagan accepted the principle that the Soviet government and its leadership represented a lawful regime with which the United States was prepared to have diplomatic dealings on issues of mutual concern.

Explicit evidence of U.S. adherence to the practices of limited linkage and rhetorical restraint came at the first meeting between Reagan and Gorbachev on October 11, 1986. Gorbachev proposed an agenda that would begin with discussion of arms reductions and shift later to regional, humanitarian, and other issues. Reagan agreed to the agenda, stressing that human rights needed to be discussed, not because the parties were to sign any agreement on the subject, but because Soviet behavior affected public opinion, and public opinion affected the degree to which the United States could work with the Soviet side. Reagan's purpose here was to make clear that Soviet concessions on human rights issues made progress on arms reduction easier to achieve politically, but that the United States would not formally link the two areas and would not use human rights progress as a basis for concessions on strategic issues. The United States would not advance such issues as demands, Reagan said, and "would never take credit for this,"[13] thereby assuring Gorbachev that no triumphal statements would follow Soviet humanitarian acts. During the morning meeting on October 12, when the leaders agreed briefly to discuss humanitarian issues, Reagan repeated these

12. MOC, 10:00 am–1:35 pm, Oct. 12, 1986, pp. 18–19.
13. MOC, 10:40 am–12:30 pm, Oct. 11, 1986, p. 2.

points, making very clear that the United States would not resort to public pressure by linking these issues and would not exploit any concessions. This is summarized in the Memorandum of Conversation as follows:

> The President . . . had no intention of saying publicly that he had demanded anything from Gorbachev in terms of such issues as family reunification and religious persecution. But he did want to urge Gorbachev to move forward in this area, since it was a major factor domestically in limiting how far the President could go in cooperation with the Soviet Union. . . . We would continue to provide lists of people we had reason to believe wanted to depart. And if the Soviets loosened up, we would not exploit it. We would simply express our appreciation.[14]

The results of the principled and disciplined manner in which the United States pursued its objectives with the Soviet Union, at Reykjavik and thereafter, were impressive. Despite their failure to agree on a comprehensive package at Reykjavik, a year later President Reagan and Secretary Gorbachev signed a treaty eliminating intermediate-range missiles. Negotiations continued on the same basis under President George H. W. Bush, who completed the START I Treaty in 1991; under President Bill Clinton, who completed START II in 1993 and sought a START III treaty with deeper reductions; and under President George W. Bush, who signed the 2002 Moscow Treaty establishing ceilings of 1,700 to 2,200 operationally deployed warheads for each state, down from more than 10,000 each in 1986. The Nunn-Lugar Threat Reduction program has dismantled and destroyed or secured nuclear ma-

---

14. MOC, 10:00 am–1:35 pm, Oct. 12, 1986, p. 18.

terials; the major restraint on progress in this effort has been funds, not any failure of the parties to implement their understandings.

Future progress in achieving disarmament and international security, especially with regard to nuclear weapons and missiles, will be far more complicated even than the situation Reagan and Gorbachev faced in 1986. To what extent does the United States currently apply the negotiating legacy of Reykjavik in dealing with actual or potential enemies, that is, firm pressure on all issues, along with diplomacy based on the principles of regime acceptance, limited linkage, and restrained rhetoric? And to what extent should this legacy be followed in dealing with current threats?

The Reykjavik Legacy and Current Negotiating Policies

We cannot equate the states to which the United States currently limits its negotiating efforts or the problems such efforts pose, with the Soviet Union under Gorbachev and the issues he and Reagan addressed. Nonetheless, it is a fact that the United States does not currently conduct its relations with governments whose policies it strongly disapproves on the basis of regime acceptance, limited linkage, or rhetorical restraint.

In recent years, it has become commonplace for the U.S. government to declare—sometimes with the explicit support of Congress—that a given regime is unacceptable and must be replaced. In some instances, Congress has provided funds for the specific purpose of supporting regime change in particular states. This approach appears to be the product of frustration in dealing with complex and difficult problems, rather than of any empirical evidence that the policy of regime change is so often successful that it should become a regular method for dealing with enemies or opponents. In fact, none of the regimes that the United States has insisted should be "changed" has failed to outlast all the U.S. regimes that have indulged in this policy, except the two that were removed by force (Sadaam Hussein in Iraq and the Taliban in Afghanistan). The change in Libya's policies, though not its regime, is often cited as evidence that a tough, no-talk line can produce results. But the historical record is clear that negotiations with Libya, led by the British, Saudis, and others, prepared the ground for Qadhafi's change of course; and he, too, was ultimately affected far more by multilateral sanctions and the use of force in Iraq than by our refusal to engage him diplomatically.

It should hardly be surprising that regime change is a policy calculated to prevent diplomatic engagement. Whether explicit or implicit, calls for regime change and actual support of activities intended to bring down a particular regime are a threat to the parties and people in power in the states involved. Warnings that the United States seeks regime change tend to strongly convey the threat that force may someday be used. For example, Assistant Secretary Christopher Hill recently said that the North Korean regime can "have a future or nuclear weapons, but not both,"[15] and declared on October 4, 2006, that "we are not going to live with a nuclear North Korea."[16] These statements—and many similar ones issued with regard to Iran and other states—are understood by these states as a warning that the United States will at some point insist on and enforce its desired outcome, without negotiating in order to make that outcome a reality. If it were clear that this form of negotiation is in fact likely to be followed by the use of force if necessary,

15. Christopher Hill, "Inaugural Address of the U.S.-Korea Institute" (The Johns Hopkins Paul H. Nitze School of Advanced International Studies, Washington, D.C., October 4, 2006).

16. David E. Sanger, "U.S. Weighs Sanctions Against North Korea," *New York Times* (October 6, 2006), http://www.nytimes.com/2006/10/06/world/asia/06nuke.html (accessed October 9, 2006).

the technique would have credibility despite the resentment it appears to provoke. But the well-known costs, to the United States, South and North Korea, and other states that could be affected by a military effort to end this threat, and the limited appetite that now exists in Congress and among the American people for such a venture have caused some observers—and perhaps even the states to which such threats are directed— to view such statements as posturing in the hope that the regimes involved will change course due to pressures and considerations brought to bear by activities other than bilateral negotiations. Forcing Iran to comply with U.S. demands is, if anything, likely to be even more costly and less likely to succeed than doing so with North Korea.

Simultaneously with issuing frequent calls for regime change, the United States has recently used linkage liberally as a basis for refusing to negotiate. In rejecting North Korea's offer of talks in November 2002, the administration's spokesman said: "It's not a question of talking. It's a question of action."[17] This echoes Secretary of State Condoleezza Rice's recent statement explaining why talks with Syria were unnecessary: "Syria knows what it has to do."[18] After years of refusing to participate in negotiations with Iran, the United States has agreed to do so, but only if Iran first suspends its uranium enrichment activities. The premise here appears to be that a refusal to negotiate is more likely to produce the desired behavior than negotiation. This may not be so. It is also argued that a particular negotiation would be futile or would harm either the prestige or interests of the United States

17. Quoted in Philip Shenon, "White House Rejects North Korean Offer for Talks," *New York Times* (Nov. 4, 2002), p. A10.

18. U.S. Secretary of State Condoleezza Rice press conference remarks at the London Meeting on the Support of the Palestinian Authority, March 8, 2005; in "Syria Under Attack," *Al-Ahram Weekly*, no. 732 (March 3–9, 2005).

more than continued stalemate or the most harmful adverse outcome. These claims are often unfounded, ultimately because negotiations need not cost anything and because they can be arranged at levels or on terms that avoid embarrassment or harmful consequences.

Secretary of State Colin Powell's statement, "You can't eat plutonium,"[19] suggested that North Korea would ultimately get reasonable in order to get food; but the leadership there appears to be well enough fed to endure the hardships their powerless citizens are facing. Indeed, Powell's premise may be flawed, since President Kim Jong Il may have concluded that making plutonium and fashioning it into bombs is in fact his regime's best meal ticket and the most valuable thing he will ever have for sale. Syria may well have an analogous reaction to warnings that it will get no help in starting a negotiation with Israel to get back the Golan Heights until it stops supporting Hezbollah in Lebanon, Hamas in Gaza, and Al Qaeda in Iraq. Syria may believe, however, after some forty years of failing to reacquire control of its sovereign lands, that only through disruptive conduct, and perhaps ultimately a war with Israel (as futile but as effective as Egypt's attack in 1973), will it succeed in this aim. One cannot know without engaging Syria on the issues what it actually thinks and how it would respond to effective diplomacy that presents it with a credible alternative to misconduct.

It is also clear that in dealing with current threats, the United States has escalated its rhetoric. Calling North Korea, Syria, and Iran an "axis of evil" is neither inaccurate nor inconsistent with successful diplomacy. Such statements are likely to offend, but do not necessarily prevent the United

19. Quoted in David E. Sanger, "Next Question: How to Stop Nuclear Blackmail," *New York Times* (Mar. 9, 2002), Week in Review, p. 1.

States from negotiating effectively if advanced as the U.S. view of certain conduct that it disapproves. In the context of a refusal to negotiate, such statements are more likely to be regarded as the warning of a determination to overthrow those regimes, just as the Axis Powers were overthrown, through any means, including force. Repeated, public announcements that the United States will not tolerate Iran having a nuclear weapon and that Iran must stop all enrichment activities or face an escalation of international pressure are forcing Iran into decisions that translate domestically and internationally into its having given in to or resisted, U.S. pressure. The United States is currently negotiating with North Korea and Iran through a process based wholly on public pronouncements, leaving direct negotiations to its allies and international officials. A routine has developed in which the United States announces what it expects to be achieved in a round of negotiations conducted by others, and the consequences it intends to pursue through the Security Council or otherwise if it considers the result of that round insufficient. Any decision by North Korea or Iran to move in a direction supported by the United States will, in this context, be seen as something the United States has accomplished through pressure. The dim prospects of success in such a negotiating context are heightened, moreover, by the fact that these open, ongoing confrontations are focused exclusively on the nuclear issue and therefore cannot benefit from agreements on unrelated, more tractable issues that are usually possible in normal negotiating contexts.

Conclusion

The negotiating legacy of U.S.-Soviet arms control efforts, dramatically evidenced by the fact that the Reykjavik meeting occurred and by its significant and positive consequences, suggest that successful diplomacy with hostile governments begins with determined pressure against their misconduct, unflinchingly applied. The pressures must be real, however, and their effects need to be exploited through engagement based on rules that permit U.S. efforts to succeed. It may be no coincidence that this administration, like President Reagan's, has had great successes in its diplomatic efforts when it has engaged directly and robustly, as with China, India, Eastern Europe, and elsewhere. The facts that the United States is able to act as an effective bridge between India and Pakistan and that it remains the most effective mediating force in the Middle East indicate that it is not for lack of skill or capacity that U.S. diplomacy with regard to hostile regimes has been relatively ineffective.

Where regime change is the only option and is feasible, the challenges that face the United States are to obtain international legitimacy for removing the regime involved and for doing so successfully. Where regime change is not the only option, however, then regime acceptance is the ticket of admission to the diplomatic process that must be undertaken. If, as with the Soviets, the regime involved is acting badly in several areas—supporting terrorism, for example, or assisting in the spread of nuclear weapons or missile technology—linking those subjects to a willingness to discuss issues the United States needs to discuss will make negotiations unlikely if not impossible. Linkage may in some instances succeed in achieving results, but it often prevents the United States from pursuing important objectives of its own. Finally, rhetoric has its place, especially to express the moral and political principles that underlie U.S. positions. But rhetoric is no substitute for real pressure, and it can make it more difficult for the United States to evoke desired conduct and is therefore ineffective diplomacy.

Six-Country Concept for a Multilateral Mechanism for Reliable Access to Nuclear Fuel

James Timbie
Presented September 21, 2006, by Jim Timbie on behalf of France, Germany, Russia, the Netherlands, the United Kingdom, and the United States

AS WE HAVE HEARD this morning, nuclear energy will play an essential role in meeting growing energy demand and supporting sustainable development. We share the goal of meeting this increasing demand for nuclear energy and nuclear technology while preventing proliferation of nuclear weapons.

As we also heard this morning, fuel supply assurances have been discussed for decades as an incentive to enable countries to enjoy the benefits of nuclear energy without indigenous sensitive fuel cycle facilities. With the prospect of the development of nuclear energy programs in a number of countries in the coming years, we have a collective responsibility to address nonproliferation in an appropriate manner, without questioning the rights and obligations that are an important part of the Nuclear Non-Proliferation Treaty (NPT) and the nuclear nonproliferation regime.

An impressive amount of study has been devoted to this subject. More than thirty years ago, the International Nuclear Fuel Cycle Evaluation project advocated a safety net and an

Jim Timbie has a Ph.D. in physics and is Senior Adviser to the Under Secretary of State for Arms Control and International Security. He has served in senior advisory positions in the State Department on arms control and nuclear issues since 1971.

international fuel bank. Two key suggestions of the 2005 report of the Director General's Expert Group on Multilateral Approaches to the Nuclear Fuel Cycle are a virtual fuel bank and a physical fuel bank—the same ideas, expressed today in the language of the Internet.

Despite a considerable amount of work and development of creative ideas over an extended period of time, there is nothing now in place for the international community to provide help for a country starting out in nuclear power should it encounter a problem with nuclear fuel supply.

The Director General has called the dissemination of sensitive fuel cycle technology the Achilles' heel of the nonproliferation regime and has identified reliable access to fuel as a way to remove the incentive for indigenous fuel cycle capabilities.

Our intent is to provide an incentive for countries to voluntarily choose not to pursue enrichment and reprocessing.

We agree with the report of the Expert Group that the commercial market is healthy and is a reliable and economical source of nuclear fuel. The goal is to create an additional incentive to rely on the commercial market and not pursue enrichment and reprocessing capabilities by establishing a mechanism to resolve any supply problems that may arise in the future so there is no need to hedge by investing in indigenous facilities. Reactor operators would have new options for arranging a secure supply of nuclear fuel.

Our concept has multiple components. Any single measure would not be sufficient, but the combination can provide assurance that a fuel disruption would be appropriately addressed.

The six states involved in supply of enrichment services and enriched uranium have been working together to make the transition from years of study to taking the first concrete steps to establish such a mechanism. To achieve real results, we propose to proceed step-by-step.

The first step would be to put in place a mechanism that would be useful, even if it would not solve all problems. Subsequent steps would gradually become more comprehensive. To simplify the problem, we propose to deal initially with supply of enriched uranium, with the intention of addressing other more difficult elements, like spent fuel management, in subsequent steps.

Our concept involves several tiers:

- The first tier is the commercial market, which is currently functioning reliably and efficiently. Our approach is designed so as not to disrupt the existing market. Assurances would be a backup mechanism.

- The next tier would be the establishment of a fuel supply assurance mechanism at the International Atomic Energy Agency (IAEA). If commercial supply arrangements are interrupted for reasons other than questions about nonproliferation obligations and cannot be restored through normal commercial processes, a country could approach the IAEA and seek help through the mechanism.

In other words, if the supply problem is a consequence of questions about compliance with NPT obligations, the mechanism could not be used. If the problem can be resolved commercially, the mechanism could also not be used.

Under this mechanism, the IAEA would assess whether the country in question has comprehensive safeguards and an additional protocol in place, any safeguards implementation issues outstanding, and appropriate safety and physical protection standards and whether it has chosen to obtain fuel on the international market and not to pursue sensitive fuel cycle activities. If these conditions are met, the IAEA could seek to facilitate new arrangements with new suppliers, with the cooperation of supplier states and companies.

The concept includes commitments by supplier states. These commitments are necessarily qualified by each state's laws and regulations. We and other suppliers cannot make unqualified commitments concerning what we will and won't do many years in the future. Supplier states can and would commit, in principle, to endeavor to allow exports of enriched uranium in implementation of the mechanism and to avoid opposing exports by others.

Another tier would involve mutual backup arrangements by commercial companies, to substitute for each other in the event of problems. These arrangements would be entered into by the commercial suppliers and purchasers themselves; we would welcome and facilitate them.

A final tier, envisioned as a last resort, would be the establishment of reserves of enriched uranium. Secretary Bodman announced at the General Conference last year that the United States will convert up to seventeen tons of highly enriched uranium excess to our national security needs into low enriched uranium to create a reserve to back up fuel supply assurances.

We see benefits in diversity and encourage others to create such reserves. We think a reserve administered by the IAEA would have important advantages, and in this regard, we welcome and support the initiative put forward by Senator Sam Nunn this morning to establish such a reserve.

The fuel supply mechanism could be developed and strengthened over time, proceeding in a step-by-step manner rather than waiting for a solution for all problems for all time. We recognize the logic of extending the benefits of the mechanism to back-end issues, which would be more complex and difficult, in a future step.

President Putin of Russia has proposed to establish an international center that would focus initially on the provision of uranium enrichment services, based on one of its existing enrichment plants. We welcome and support this proposal. The Russian approach and our concept would complement each other and be mutually supportive.

The concept put forward by the six was discussed at the June 2006 Board meeting. Although there was support, concerns were also expressed. Some argued against it on the grounds that rights to nuclear technology should not be restricted.

The mechanism would be implemented on a voluntary basis. There is no intent to take away any rights of any states. There is no suggestion that states should give up rights under Article IV of the NPT.

Countries starting out in nuclear energy have choices. They can choose to have only reactors or to have fuel cycle facilities as well. Both choices are available under the NPT. We are seeking to provide an incentive to choose to have nuclear energy but not to have sensitive fuel cycle technologies. We are not asking for any commitment in advance.

If a supply problem should arise in the future, use of the mechanism would be voluntary. The mechanism would be available to any state meeting established criteria and which has voluntarily chosen to obtain fuel on the commercial market and not pursue indigenous sensitive fuel cycle facilities. The intent is to enable states to reliably enjoy the benefits of nuclear energy without the costs of fuel cycle facilities while discouraging the spread of sensitive technologies.

The countries we see benefiting from this mechanism would be developed and developing countries, looking to nuclear energy to support clean development, enabling them to move forward relying on the commercial market backed up by a multilateral mechanism they could turn to in the event of a supply problem.

We welcome this Special Event and thank the IAEA for calling it to focus international attention and energy on this important issue. We are hopeful that as a result of this Special Event, the international community will return to this issue with renewed energy to put in place soon a fuel supply assurance mechanism that has been the subject of much study and discussion.

We stand ready to work further with the Secretariat and with other member states to develop this concept together with other compatible ideas that were put forward this morning, particularly the legal and technical and economic aspects, as part of the way forward following this Special Event.

Appendix One

Memorandum
of
Conversation

Transcripts of the discussions of
President Ronald Reagan and
Secretary of State George P.
Shultz with General Secretary
Mikhail Gorbachev and Foreign
Minister Eduard Shevardnadze

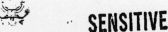

CHRON FILE
United States Department of State
SYSTEM II
Washington. D.C. 20520 90725

SENSITIVE

~~SECRET~~ MEMORANDUM OF CONVERSATION

DATE: October 11, 1986

TIME: 10:40 a.m. – 12:30 p.m.

PARTICIPANTS:

US SIDE

President Reagan
Secretary Shultz (came in at 11:30)
Ambassador Matlock
D. Zarechnak (interpreter)

USSR SIDE

General Secretary Gorbachev
Foreign Minister Shevardnadze (came in at 11:30)
Notetaker
N. Upsenskiy (interpreter)

The President invited the General Secretary to have a seat at the table.

Gorbachev thanked the President and noted that both sides had a lot of paper with them. What did this mean?

The President replied that it was to recall the things that the two of them had discussed in Geneva. He continued that he was glad that the General Secretary had proposed this meeting, since it was important to make sure that their next meeting would be a productive one.

Gorbachev replied, in turn, that he and the Soviet leadership very much appreciated the President's agreement to have this meeting.

The President said that he had been looking forward to the meeting. He proposed that the two of them could meet alone, and perhaps also alternate their meetings with meetings that would include the respective Foreign Ministers. Would the General Secretary agree to such an approach?

Gorbachev indicated that he would.

The President asked Gorbachev which questions he felt they should discuss.

~~SECRET~~ SENSITIVE

Gorbachev replied that he wished to begin with a brief exchange
of views about the present situation, which had given rise to
Gorbachev's proposal to meet with the President before his visit
to the US. After that he would tell the President about the
proposals which he had brought with him. At that point they
might ask Foreign Minister Shevardnadze and Secretary Shultz to
join them.

The President indicated that this was acceptable.

Gorbachev said that he was prepared to talk about everything that
the President thought needed to be discussed here.

The President replied that there were a number of things that had
been discussed and left open in Geneva, such as INF, the ABM
Treaty, space arms and nuclear testing. The US side was
especially interested in strategic arms proposals for the US
negotiators in Geneva. Both the US and USSR would like to see a
world without nuclear missiles. This was a very important issue,
and the world was interested in the possibility of achieving
this.

Gorbachev replied that since this was the main issue for the
meeting, perhaps they could devote this first session to that
issue, including the subsequent participation of the Foreign
Ministers. Then in the afternoon questions of regional issues,
humanitarian issues, bilateral relations, and everything else
that was the subject of mutual interest could be discussed.

The President replied that the question of humanitarian issues
and human rights needed to be discussed. This was a question
different from the other ones in that no formal agreement would
be signed on this, but this was a very important issue for the US
side. The degree to which the President could work together with
the Soviet side depended on US public opinion. This concerned
such issues as emigration. This would never be put forward as a
demand by the US side. The President was simply trying to say
how important this issue was and how it would open up greater
possibilities for achieving other aims if steps were taken along
these lines. But the US would never take credit for this.

Gorbachev suggested that after a brief exchange about how to
structure their meeting they could have a basic exchange of views
on what had happened since Geneva and in the world in general and
what US and Soviet concerns were at present. Then Secretary of
State Shultz and Foreign Minister Shevardnadze could be invited
to join them, at which time he could present specific arms
control proposals involving strategic offensive weapons,
medium-range forces, the ABM Treaty, nuclear testing, and all
issues of nuclear arms and the arms race.

The President agreed and indicated that the reason for bringing
up the other issues was their effect on the issue of arms

~~SECRET~~ **SENSITIVE**

control. As he had indicated in Geneva, this was not an attempt
to interfere in the internal affairs of the Soviet Union. But
public opinion was very important in the US. One-eighth of US
citizens have relatives and families with ties to the Soviet
Union. Just the other day, and the President would return to
this later, he had received a message from a US Senator whose
mother had emigrated from Russia. Now her son had become an
American Senator. Another example of such ties were the
President's own ties to Ireland. In general, Americans have a
very strong bond to the lands of their heritage. So it is easier
for the US to reach agrements with the USSR if public opinion is
not aroused by things that happen in the countries where people
came from. But the President agreed that the issue of nuclear
arms was the most important issue in the world today.

Gorbachev indicated that he wished to give his evaluation and the
evaluation of the Soviet leadership concerning the importance of
their present meeting in light of the current world situation as
the Soviet side sees it.

The President agreed to listen to what Gorbachev had to say.

Gorbachev stressed that much had been said in the world about the
decision to meet in Reykjavik. Many contradictory views were
being presented. But he was certain that this was an important
step which the President and the Soviet leadership had taken.
Cooperation between the US and the Soviet Union was continuing
and the present meeting bore witness to that. The process was a
difficult one and was not going as smoothly as the two countries
and their peoples might wish, but it was continuing. This was
the main thing which justified this meeting.

The President agreed.

Gorbachev continued that many people in the world viewed
the meeting between them as a chance for each of them to promote
their personal ambitions, but he totally rejected this notion and
considered that they were accountable vis-a-vis their governments
and their countries, since too much depended on the two
countries, the relationship between them, and contacts between
their two leaders.

The President replied that, as he had indicated in Geneva, they
had a unique opportunity to possibly decide whether or not there
should be war or peace in the world, and he assumed that both
sides wanted peace. The question was how to bring this about
with confidence and with a decrease in mistrust between the two
peoples.

Gorbachev said that this was his second thought as well. Since
Geneva the development of the bilateral relationship had not been
smooth, and there were occasional flair-ups. The relationship
was not an easy one, but it had been improving. But with regard

to the main issue, which was of greatest concern, i.e., the
nuclear threat, the Geneva Summit had been intended to give a
push to the negotiations on this issue. A great deal has been
said about the matter, but that things had come to an impasse.
For when there are 50 or 100 different proposals, there is no
commonality of approach and no indication of progress. For this
reason Gorbachev felt that a meeting was necessary in order to
push the two sides along the main directions aimed at achieving
agreements which could be signed during Gorbachev's visit to the
US.

The President replied that these were the thoughts of the US
Delegation as well. After Geneva, the experts of both sides had
presented various proposals. The US side had presented a
proposal for 50 percent reduction, which was apparently too much
for the Soviet side. The US had proposed a limit of 4500 on
ballistic missile warheads, and the Soviet side had proposed 6400
to 6800. The US side felt that this number was too high and that
with such a high level, the world would still be threatened by
destruction. The US, however, was ready to conclude an interim
agreement, and bearing in mind the goal of total elimination of
such weapons, the US would be prepared to agree to a number
between those two figures, i.e., 5500.

Gorbachev replied that he wished to make it very clear to the
President and the US Government that the Soviet side wished to
find such solutions which would take equal account of Soviet and
US interests. Any other approach would not be realistic. If the
Soviet side only wished to look out for its interests or to
strive for superiority in some other way, it felt that this would
not stimulate US interest. An agreement could not be built on
such a basis. He wanted to clearly say that the Soviet side was
in favor of proposals which were aimed at total elimination of
nuclear arms, and on the way to this goal there should be
equality and equal security for the Soviet Union and the United
States. Any other approach would not be acceptable. The Soviet
side would count on the President and the US Government to
approach the situation in the same way.

The President indicated his agreement and added that one of the
most difficult issues of the negotiations was the issue of
verification, to make sure that both sides did what they had
promised to do. He quoted a Russian proverb: "Doveryay no
proveryay (trust but verify)." In previous statements, the two
sides had spoken optimistically about INF and the eventual
elimination of nuclear weapons. The negotiators in Geneva had
discussed a cut-back in the number of weapons. And whether the
two sides would start there or would start with proposals to
decrease strategic weapons, if agreement could be reached on
verification which would give confidence about the fact that
neither side was doing what it had agreed not to, this could be a
very big step, and the world would cheer.

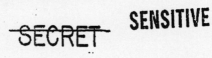

SENSITIVE

~~SECRET~~

Gorbachev replied that he would like to support what the
President had said about the importance of verification. The two
sides were now at the stage where they could begin a concrete
process aimed at arriving at agreements, and verification had an
important part to play in this. The Soviet side was interested
in this issue. Without such verification he did not think it
would be possible to have agreements leading to greater peace and
an improvement of the international situation. The Soviet side
was prepared, and he knew that the US was also prepared, to go as
far as necessary to have complete confidence in the fact that
agreements were being fulfilled.

Gorbachev said that he wished to say one more thing and then
Secretary Shultz and Foreign Minister Shevardnadze could be
invited in and he could present the Soviet side's specific
proposals. He wished to touch upon their next meeting in the US.
Reykjavik was sort of half-way point on the way to that meeting.

The President agreed.

Gorbachev said that someone had stated that Iceland was picked
because it was the same distance from Moscow and Washington and
that this was done in order to show that the US and USSR were
working on the basis of equality in every respect.

The President replied that he had chosen Iceland out of the
proposals made by the General Secretary not because he had
measured the distances, but because he felt that London was too
big and too busy a city and would not lend itself to the type of
free discussions which they wished to have. He then asked
Gorbachev if he had a date in mind for the U.S. meeting or
whether he, the President, ought to propose a date.

Gorbachev replied that, as he had written to the President and as
he had stated publicly, the Soviet side felt that the meeting in
the US should be marked by concrete results on important issues,
primarily those concerning halting the arms race, which were of
concern to the US people, the Soviet people and other nations as
well. That meeting could not be permitted to fail. This would
have very serious consequences. The world would say that these
politicians are meeting and talking, which was good, but a great
deal of time had been spent and there had been one meeting, two
meetings, and three meetings without any forward movement. This
would be very bad for the two countries and for the world. So
the present meeting should lay a basis for the meeting in the US
during which specific agreements could be signed. After there is
an exchange of views and the two sides see where they are and how
they should work in order to arrive at agreements to be finalized
in the US, what instructions are to be given and how much work
needs to be done, then the two sides could agree on the date of
the meeting.

The President agreed and said that they could go forward and try

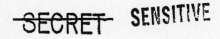

~~SECRET~~ SENSITIVE

to achieve such understandings. He indicated, however, that in talking about the number of missiles, he had failed to mention one important factor, i.e., an agreement on throw-weight. It would not be good if there were agreement only on the number of missiles where one side had considerably more destructive power. As he had indicated before, this would be an element of an interim step on the way to complete elimination of nuclear weapons.

Gorbachev noted that exactly one hour had passed during which they had exchanged views on the basic relationship, and if the President did not object, they might now call in their Foreign Ministers, and he would like to give the US side the Soviet side's proposals on nuclear weapons.

The President agreed.

After a short interval, Secretary Shultz and Foreign Minister Shevardnadze joined the President and the General Secretary.

The President explained to Secretary Shultz that the General Secretary had started by speaking of strategic missiles and had indicated that various figures had been given in Geneva. The proposals which the Soviet side has come with would be aimed at producing results which could then be finalized and signed during the next meeting between the President and the General Secretary in the United States.

Gorbachev said that if the President did not object, he wanted to present the Soviet side's proposals, which would then give a push to the negotiators in Geneva.

The President agreed to listen to Gorbachev's proposals.

Gorbachev indicated that in the basic exchange of opinions on bilateral relations, he had recognized an admission of the mutual ultimate aim of total elimination of nuclear weapons. This stemmed from what had been agreed in Geneva, i.e., that a nuclear war must never be fought. On January 15 the Soviet side had proposed a plan for the complete elimination of nuclear weapons. The US side had also made various proposals. Gorbachev wished to confirm that the US side should understand that during the movement towards complete elimination of nuclear weapons, it was expected that there would be equality and equal security for both sides at all stages of this process. Neither side should attempt to strive to achieve superiority.

Gorbachev said that he wanted to begin with the area of strategic offensive weapons. In Geneva the Soviet side had proposed a reduction of these weapons by 50 percent. Since then, and at present, many different options have been floated in Geneva, but now he wished to say that the Soviet side is interested in

radical reductions of strategic offensive arms by 50 percent and
no less. In the year's time that had gone by since Geneva the
Soviet side had become convinced that it would be possible to
expect large reductions in these systems.

Gorbachev continued that, unlike previous Soviet proposals,
wherein the 50 percent covered all weapons reaching the territory
of the other side, the present one concerns only strategic
weapons, without including medium-range missiles or forward-based
systems. This takes into account the US viewpoint and is a
concession.

Gorbachev continued that since strategic arms formed the basis of
the nuclear might of the two sides, it would be especially
important to have a good understanding of each other's interests
and to have equality. As had been indicated before, historically
the composition of the nuclear forces of the two sides has been
different. Nevertheless, in reducing these forces by 50 percent,
the Soviet side would be prepared to have a considerable
reduction of heavy missiles, in answer to US concerns. He wished
to stress that this would be considerable, and not just cosmetic.
However, he would expect the US side to have the same regard for
the Soviet side's concerns. One example of this would be the
fact that there are now 6500 nuclear warheads on American
submarines which are all over the world and which are difficult
to monitor. More than 800 of these missiles are MIRVed. The
Soviet side knows the great precision of US missiles, both
submarine-based and land-based. Therefore, each side would need
to meet the concerns of the other one, and not to try to back it
into a corner.

Gorbachev continued that with regard to medium-range missiles, a
great deal has been said lately between the two countries and in
the world. Various predictions are being made even as the two of
them sat here together. The Soviet side had analyzed this issue
again, taking into consideration the situation in Western Europe,
the views of governments there, as well as public opinion, and
had decided to take a broad approach on this issue. Solutions
ought to be found which would take account of the interests of
the two sides, as well as their allies. Therefore, the Soviet
side was proposing to have a complete elimination of US and
Soviet medium-range nuclear forces in Europe. In doing so, the
Soviet side has made the concession not to count English and
French nuclear forces. This was a big step, since both
quantitatively and qualitatively the possibilities of developing
those forces were very great. But a compromise needed to be
found, and therefore risks needed to be taken.

Gorbachev continued that with regard to medium-range nuclear
forces in Asia, in the spirit of cooperation and in light of the
concessions made by the Soviet side, the US should take back its
demands about these missiles or give instructions to both sides
to negotiate this issue, i.e, nuclear forces in Asia - both

The President continued that the US side believed that the Soviet
side was also doing research on defensive systems. The US side
was proposing in this new treaty to go forward with development,
staying within the ABM limits, and when the point was reached when
testing was required beyond the limits of the ABM Treaty, the US
would go forward with such testing in the presence of
representatives of the other country. So if the US side were
first in developing such a system, the Soviet side would observe
the test. If testing showed that such a defense system could be
practical, then the treaty would call for the US to share this
defense system. In return for this, there would be a total
elimination of strategic missiles. A two year period could be set
for negotiating this elimination of strategic missiles and the
sharing of the defense system.

The President continued that the reason for wanting such a system
was that the two of them would not be there forever. Perhaps in
the future there might be those who would want to cheat or there
might be a madman such as Hitler who would want to have such
weapons. But if both countries had such a defense system, we
would not need to be concerned about what others might do and we
could rid the world of strategic nuclear arms. Such a treaty
would be signed by both sides and would be binding on both sides
for the future as well.

Gorbachev indicated that he wished to briefly reply to what the
President had said. First of all, he thought that the President's
reply was a preliminary one, since these were new proposals by the
Soviet side which had not been put forward before. He asked the
President to study them, and they could meet again to have an
exchange on this. The things that the President had said now had
already been mentioned on the level of the negotiators in Geneva.
The Soviet side valued the work which the specialists were doing
in Geneva, but at the present talks a push needed to be given to
those negotiators, and it was for this reason that the Soviet side
had made its proposals.

Gorbachev continued that the Soviet side had proposed to agree to
the US zero option with regard to medium-range missiles and was
ready to discuss the question of the missiles in Asia. But the
President had gone back on his previous proposals, and the Soviet
side did not understand this.

Gorbachev continued that with regard to the ABM Treaty, the Soviet
side's proposal concerned a very important instrument which needed
to be preserved. The US side, on the other hand, wanted to
renounce the ABM Treaty.

Gorbachev continued that with regard to SDI, the Soviet side had
sorted this out and was not concerned about the creation of a
three-tier ABM system by the US. It would have a reply to such a
system. The Soviet side was concerned about something else, i.e.,
moving the arms race into a new stage and into a new medium, and

complete cessation of such tests. There have been negotiations
on this before. The Soviet side was proposing to the US to
renew either bilateral or trilateral negotiations (together with
the British) in order to get agreement on a comprehensive test
ban. During these negotiations, each side could do what it
wished about testing, but the Soviet side felt that during the
negotiations, the sides could look at questions of verification,
lowering of thresholds, decreasing the number of nuclear
explosions, and the 1974 and 1976 treaties. Renewing the CTB
negotiations would be a good beginning and would be helpful for
quickly arriving at an agreement on strategic missile forces.

Gorbachev concluded that this was the package of Soviet
proposals. He wanted to suggest that the two of them give
instructions to the appropriate agencies, for example, the
Ministry of Foreign Affairs and the Department of State, to
produce a draft agreement for signature in the US. In the
context of these proposals, the Soviet side was interested in
effective verification and was prepared to implement such
verification by any means necessary, including on-site
inspection, and would expect the same of the US side. Since
these were very serious issues, in order to exclude the
possibility of any misinterpretation, h e said he now wished to
pass these proposals in writing, in English, to the President.

The President replied that the General Secretary's proposals
were very encouraging, although there were some diffeences
vis-a-vis the US position. The first one concerned INF. The
zero proposal in Europe was acceptable, but the missiles in Asia
should also be reduced, because these missiles could be targeted
on Europe, and the allies would be left without a deterrent.
After consultation with Secretary Shultz, the President said
that instead of the zero option, there could be a maximum of 100
warheads on each side. In this case, there would still be a
NATO deterrent left. But the main issue was strategic arms.
The US side also wants to reduce them to zero. But there is a
problem with the question of the ABM provisions. SDI was born
as an idea which would give a chance to all of us to completely
eliminate strategic weapons. The US side proposed to go forward
in reducing the number of strategic weapons and to sign a treaty
which would supersede the ABM Treaty.

SENSITIVE

SECRET

The President continued that the US side believed that the Soviet
side was also doing research on defensive systems. The US side
was proposing in this new treaty to go forward with development,
staying within the ABM limits, and when the point was reached when
testing was required beyond the limits of the ABM Treaty, the US
would go forward with such testing in the presence of
representatives of the other country. So if the US side were
first in developing such a system, the Soviet side would observe
the test. If testing showed that such a defense system could be
practical, then the treaty would call for the US to share this
defense system. In return for this, there would be a total
elimination of strategic missiles. A two year period could be set
for negotiating this elimination of strategic missiles and the
sharing of the defense system.

The President continued that the reason for wanting such a system
was that the two of them would not be there forever. Perhaps in
the future there might be those who would want to cheat or there
might be a madman such as Hitler who would want to have such
weapons. But if both countries had such a defense system, we
would not need to be concerned about what others might do and we
could rid the world of strategic nuclear arms. Such a treaty
would be signed by both sides and would be binding on both sides
for the future as well.

Gorbachev indicated that he wished to briefly reply to what the
President had said. First of all, he thought that the President's
reply was a preliminary one, since these were new proposals by the
Soviet side which had not been put forward before. He asked the
President to study them, and they could meet again to have an
exchange on this. The things that the President had said now had
already been mentioned on the level of the negotiators in Geneva.
The Soviet side valued the work which the specialists were doing
in Geneva, but at the present talks a push needed to be given to
those negotiators, and it was for this reason that the Soviet side
had made its proposals.

Gorbachev continued that the Soviet side had proposed to agree to
the US zero option with regard to medium-range missiles and was
ready to discuss the question of the missiles in Asia. But the
President had gone back on his previous proposals, and the Soviet
side did not understand this.

Gorbachev continued that with regard to the ABM Treaty, the Soviet
side's proposal concerned a very important instrument which needed
to be preserved. The US side, on the other hand, wanted to
renounce the ABM Treaty.

Gorbachev continued that with regard to SDI, the Soviet side had
sorted this out and was not concerned about the creation of a
three-tier ABM system by the US. It would have a reply to such a
system. The Soviet side was concerned about something else, i.e.,
moving the arms race into a new stage and into a new medium, and

-11-

creating new weapons ~~which would destabilize the strategic~~
~~situation in the world~~. If this was what the US Administration
wanted, that was one thing. But if the US Administration wanted
greater security for the American people and its allies, then SDI
was dangerous.

Gorbachev wished to end his quick reply to what the President had
said, but asked the President to carefully examine the new Soviet
proposals and to answer them point by point, with indication of
where US agreed and where it had problems. This was important
for the Soviet side and he thought it was important for the US
side as well. He noticed that it seemed to be time to end the
meeting.

The President said that he wished to say one thing. The two
sides would discuss these things after lunch, and the US side
would review the Soviet proposals. But he thought that the
Soviet side was refusing to see the point of SDI. If US research
showed that there could be such a system, and if the US went
forward with such a system in the presence of offensive systems,
then it could be accused of striving for a first-strike
capability, since it had both protection and offensive arms. But
the US would forego this. The treaty he had proposed would
prevent the deployment of such a system until there was complete
elimination of nuclear weapons. At the same time this system
would be available to both sides, and would not be deployed until
there was a complete elimination of nuclear weapons.

The President continued that the General Secretary might ask why,
in that case, was there a need for defensive arms at all. And
the answer was that the world knows how to make offensive arms,
and just as we kept our gas masks after World War I in case there
would ever be a temptation to use gas warfare in the future, such
a system would be in place in case there was the temptation to
secretly build nuclear missiles after the world had gotten rid of
them. But this could be discussed further after lunch.

Gorbachev replied that a year had passed since their meeting in
Geneva, and the Soviet side had studied the question of SDI very
carefully and had sorted it out. He had indicated the Soviet
side's view to the President.

Gorbachev asked the President if they should continue to discuss
these issues in the afternoon, or go on to other ones.

The President replied that they should go on to other ones.

Draft:DZarechnak:jms

CHRON FILE
SYSTEM II
90725

MEMORANDUM OF CONVERSATION

Date: October 11, 1986
Time: 3:30 PM - 5:40 PM
Place: Hofdi House, Reykjavik

PARTICIPANTS

US Side   Soviet Side

President Reagan   General Secretary Gorbachev
Secretary Shultz   Foreign Minister Shevardnadze
Tom Simons, Notetaker   G. Tarasenko, Notetaker
William Hopkins, Interpreter   P. Pavlazhchenko, Interpreter

The President recalled that Gorbachev had presented him with a paper that morning. He had not yet had a chance to digest it, and he would like to read Gorbachev a paper here, which had some suggestions at the end.

Having listened to Gorbachev's remarks in the morning, we agreed that reductions are the highest priority. It is time for practical steps. He also welcomed from Gorbachev's remarks the focus Gorbachev had placed on ballistic missiles.

Reductions in ballistic missile warheads are central, the President went on. The heart of the matter is reducing ballistic missile warheads.

We had agreed to 50% reductions and proposed 4500 ballistic missile warheads, roughly half the current Soviet level. The Soviets had proposed 6400 to 6800, and as he had said that morning, he thought that was too high.

We had been prepared to talk about lesser reductions, but we preferred to talk about 50%, as Gorbachev had that morning.

We are concerned about heavy ICBMs, the President went on, and glad to hear the Soviets were prepared for considerable reductions in these systems. (This line was omitted in the interpretation.)

We are prepared for appropriate corresponding reductions in all ballistic missile systems -- including in our sea-launched ballistic missile force (the sub-launched ballistic missiles), as the Soviets had suggested. Additionally, we need throwweight reductions, additional sublimits and effective verification.

- 1 -

- 2 -

The President elaborated that the agreement should reduce throwweight to 50% of the current Soviet level, and that effective verification is essential to both of us, and should apply the progress made in INF and other areas to what we call START.

As part of such a package, the President said, we are ready to agree in other areas.

There should be limits on air-launched cruise missiles, but not limits on other bomber weapons. We are prepared to constrain ALCMs by including them in a limit of 6000 (the interpreter said 7500) on ballistic missile warheads and ALCMs -- but not include other bomber weapons, gravity bombs and SRAM.

The President then turned to a sublimit on bombers. Bombers fly slow and face unconstrained Soviet air defenses. You cannot equate bomber weapons with missile warheads, and this was not done in past arms control agreements. But we can consider a sublimit of 350 bombers, thus bounding bomber weapons.

There should be an aggregate ceiling on bombers and ballistic missiles, the President said, and we can accept the aggregate ceiling of 1600 on ICBMs, SLBMs and heavy bombers the Soviets had proposed.

If we can work out such an agreement, the President said, it should not be held hostage to progress in other areas.

Turning to INF, the President said that with respect to Gorbachev's remarks on intermediate-range nuclear forces, he had to say he was disappointed. Gorbachev's most recent letter to him had indicated that although problems remain, we might be moving to closure in this area.

For example, in the letter Gorbachev had written to him that with regard to Soviet systems in Asia, "a mutually acceptable formula can be found and I am ready to propose one (provided there is certainty that a willingness to resolve the issue of medium-range missiles in Europe does exist)."

Gorbachev now appeared to be backing off this position, the President noted.

This issue must be dealt with on a global basis, the President went on. He had thought we had agreed to pursue an interim, global agreement. We both agreed on an interim INF agreement with equal ceilings on U.S. and Soviet long-range intermediate missile warheads in Europe, and an equal ceiling on U.S. and Soviet long-range missile warheads worldwide.

- 3 -

There should be no doubt, the President said, that we require a global solution.

We can accept the Soviet idea of 100 in Europe, he went on, if other elements are worked out. The Soviets had proposed 100 warheads on each side in Europe. If we can agree on the other aspects of an interim agreement, we have no problem with that number.

Verification is essential, the President continued. In Gorbachev's most recent letter he had said that verification is no longer a problem. The President said he assumed that Gorbachev meant that he was prepared to be constructive in finding a solution to our verification concerns.

The President also said we need reductions in Asia. As he had pointed out, the Soviets had said privately that they have a formula to propose to help resolve this issue. It would have to go beyond the formula Gorbachev had used at Vladivostok, and also beyond what he had said that morning. The President stressed that he could not accept only a freeze in current Soviet SS-20 levels in Asia.

The U.S. had long called for proportional reductions in Asia, the President recalled. If we reduce to 100 warheads in Europe, and reduce Asian systems in the same proportion, the Asian ceiling would be something like 63. But 100 in Europe and 100 in Asia is acceptable. In the right context, we could accept that.

We need to address short-range intermediate missiles, the President continued. It cannot be deferred. At a minimum this involves limiting SRINF, including a ceiling on SRINF at least at current Soviet levels, with a U.S. right to match at whatever level, and the lower the better. The Soviets had suggested this. It was in their INF draft treaty. Reluctance now to constrain these short-range systems was troublesome, he said.

The President said he welcomed the fact that Gorbachev's remarks that morning had addressed short-range warheads and indicated a willingness to freeze Soviet forces in this area.

He would not accept a ban on Pershing IIs, the President went on. We could discuss the mix of Pershing IIs and ground-launched cruise missiles, but we could not leave the Soviets with ballistic missiles in their force while we had none.

The interim treaty should also stay in force until it is replaced, the President said. The Soviets had suggested this in their May 15 draft treaty, and we supported it.

Let's settle on 100/100 now, the President urged. We are getting somewhere. The Soviets had suggested 100 LRINF

- 4 -

missiles in Europe. We have no problem with that, if the
Soviets make comparable reductions in Asia. ·If they could
not make a proportional reduction in Asia, for example to
about 60 to 65, why not 100 warheads in Europe and 100 warheads
outside Europe, with a concurrent freeze on shorter-range
systems at the current Soviet level. The President said that
the basis for an agreement is within reach.

On SRINF,.the President went on, let's agree now to
address it. Let's agree to instruct our negotiators to agree
on constraints on SRINF missiles in an interim agreement taking
into account the capabilities of these systems and the need for
a nuclear arms reductions agreement. to reflect equality between
—the U.S. and the Soviet Union.

Let's agree now on verification measures, the President
continued. We think they should include a comprehensive and
accurate exchange of data, both prior to reductions and
thereafter; and second, on-site observation of destruction down
to agreed levels; and, three, effective monitoring of the
remaining LRINF inventories and associated facilities, including
on-site inspection.

Let's put the duration issue behind us, the President urged.
Let's agree to instruct our negotiators to resolve the duration
question in a manner which ensures that the U.S. and Soviet INF
missile systems remain subject to and constrained by a legally
functioning treaty system while the sides negotiate further
reductions in these systems.

Gorbachev asked which treaty. Secretary Shultz said
an INF treaty, along the lines the Soviets had suggested earlier. The
President commented we had gotten the idea from Gorbachev.

. Turning to defense and space, the President said he had
taken Gorbachev's concerns about the U.S. SDI program into
account in his July 25 proposal.

First of all, he said, he wanted to make clear that his
proposal recognizes that the ABM Treaty is a treaty of unlimited
duration. His proposal would establish a mechanism for the two
sides to move together towards increasing reliance on defense.
It would not eliminate the ABM Treaty. As a result of the
negotiations he had proposed, some new provisions would take
precedence over certain provisions of the ABM Treaty.

His proposal would enhance strategic stability, the President
went on, while diminishing the burden we both bear of continuous
modernization and expansion of strategic offensive forces. His
proposal envisions careful management of a transition to a

- 5 -

stabilizing balance of offensive and defensive forces. His proposal would also lead to the total elimination of offensive ballistic missiles.

The President continued that he was willing to discuss Gorbachev's concerns. They fall into two categories.

Gorbachev had suggested that our defense might be used to attack the Soviet Union. He could assure Gorbachev that it is not being developed for that purpose.

Some argue, the President went on, that SDI will inevitably lead to space-based weapons with an offensive capability against earth. That's not true. The quickest, surest and most effective way to strike earth targets is with ballistic missiles. We already have agreements banning weapons of mass destruction in space. If Gorbachev had additional concerns on this subject, the President said, we are prepared to work with the Soviets to resolve them.

Second, the President continued, Gorbachev had suggested that we might launch a first strike against the Soviets and use our defenses to prevent retaliation. We don't have that capability, and that is not our objective. But Gorbachev's concern had led the President to propose a treaty now which would lead to the elimination of all offensive ballistic missiles. Once we do that, the issue of a combination of offensive and defensive forces giving one side or the other an advantage would not arise. We would have a less costly, safer and more stable relationship.

The President said we would thereby eliminate weapons which can strike in minutes and cannot be recalled. We would end once and for all the instability that results from fears of a disarming missile first strike.

Under his proposal, the President went on, defenses would reinforce the stability achieved by eliminating ballistic missiles. Defenses would also protect each of us against cheating or the ballistic missiles of third countries. The U.S. seeks above all replacement of offensive ballistic missiles with defenses in a phased manner that provides greater stability at each stage in the disarmament process.

We are even prepared to share the benefits of strategic defense, the President said. We will agree now to a Treaty committing to do so in conjunction with the elimination of ballistic missiles.

If we eliminate all offensive ballistic missiles, the President continued, our deployments could be adjusted accordingly. Our remaining forces would be far more stable. Neither bombers nor cruise missiles are suitable for surprise attack. They are slow and vulnerable to unconstrained Soviet air defenses.

- 6 -

We need to consider the timing and phasing of a transition to strategic defense, the President said. The principles which would guide the U.S. in a transition would be equity (the interpreter translated "equality") and stability at every stage.

The President pointed out that his proposal is a very significant step. It would require very serious negotiation, but he was convinced that it gave us our best chance to put the security of both our nations on a better, more stable and long-term basis.

With respect to Gorbachev's suggestions of that morning, the President said it was not clear to him what would be the subject of the negotiations Gorbachev had suggested. Would it be what we have proposed, he asked, including sharing the benefits of defenses and the elimination of ballistic missiles?

Gorbachev said he would answer that later.

Turning to nuclear testing, the President said he welcomed Gorbachev's recognition that there should be an appropriate relationship between the requirement and existence of nuclear weapons and their testing.

The President said we need essential verification improvements for the Threshold Test Ban Treaty and Peaceful Nuclear Explosions Treaty. His top priority in the nuclear testing area was to fix the defective verification protocols of these two treaties. If the Soviets could agree on Corrtex monitoring, or some other equally effective system they might propose, we would ratify these treaties, the President said.

We have told Congress we will submit them for ratification, he went on. As a symbol of the importance he placed on this area, he had formally advised Congress that he would submit the treaties for ratification when Congress convened early next year.

If there is no resolution of verification, the President continued, we will work out a reservation on ratification. He had further advised the Congress that, if the Soviets do not agree to the required verification improvements, he would ask the Senate to consent to ratification with a reservation that delays the effective time of such ratification (the interpreter translated "entry into force") until he certified that the treaties can be effectively verified.

Congress supports this approach, the President said. The Congressional leadership supports it. Gorbachev should be under no illusions that there is division on this issue within the U.S.

- 7 -

Let's agree to fix the treaties now, the President urged.
Let us make immediate progress in the nuclear testing area by
agreeing here to fix these two treaties. That would be a sound
and logical approach. Then we will move beyond the TTBT and PNET
and immediately engage in negotiations on ways to implement a
step-by-step parallel program -- in association with a program
to reduce and ultimately eliminate all nuclear weapons -- of
limiting and ultimately ending nuclear testing.

The President said he wanted to make progress. But Gorbachev
had to know that neither a test moratorium nor a comprehensive
test ban is in the cards for the foreseeable future.

Perhaps, the President concluded, we can see if we can find
common ground based on Soviet ideas and our ideas.

Turning to risk reduction, the President said he was pleased
with the progress we have made. Let's move to agreement, he
urged. He saw no reason, given the progress we had made so far,
why we cannot agree on the goal of signing a formal agreement
to establish these centers when Gorbachev came to the United States.

Turning to compliance, the President said it is essential.
Strict compliance with existing agreements is essential to make
progress on arms control. He could not stress enough how important
this is. His policy decisions regarding SALT I and SALT II were
the result of Soviet non-compliance. And Krasnoyarsk was
especially important in this regard.

In conclusion, the President said it appears that significant
progress is possible. He proposed that they both put their
experts that night. Perhaps they might meet at 8:00 right there
in Hofdi House. They could discuss all the issues the leaders
had identified: strategic offensive weapons, intermediate-range
nuclear forces, defense and space, nuclear testing. If Gorbachev
agreed to this proposal, the U.S. side would be represented by
the same group that had discussed these issues this summer:
Ambassador Nitze, Ambassador Kampelman, Mr. Perle, Ambassador
Rowny, and with Mr. Adelman replacing the two negotiators who
were absent.

Believe it or not, the President said, he had come to the end.

Gorbachev said that before he reacted, however briefly, to

- 8 -

the President's remarks, which had covered a large number of
issues, he had some questions for clarification.

His first question concerned strategic offensive missiles.
He asked whether the President agreed to his proposal about
50% reductions in this type of system. Was this correct?

The President replied, "Yes."

Gorbachev continued that if he understood correctly, the
President had mentioned 7500. This variant had been discussed
in Geneva recently, but it involved a 30% reduction.

Secretary Shultz said the right figure was 6000. Hopkins
said he had made a mistake and said 6000. The Secretary explained
that this meant 4500 and 1500, with agreement to limit ALCMs.

Addressing the President, Gorbachev said they had been
talking about one of the impasses the Geneva negotiators had
not been able to end, concerning sublimits. He had a sheet
of data on the nuclear systems of the Soviet Union and the
United States. The proposal was to reduce these by 50%, and
since this was so, he said, let us agree to reduce all the
types the Soviet Union and the U.S. have by 50%: land-based,
sea-launched and those carried by strategic bombers. The
whole arsenal would be reduced by 50%, as would all types.
The structures have evolved historically, and if we proceed
to reduce it by 50% across the board, we will reduce the level
of strategic confrontation. The structure will remain the same,
but the level will be lower, and this will be clear to everyone.
Then the disputes which have been going on for years about
limits and sublimits will be superseded by 50% reductions.
The level of confrontation will be cut in half.

He asked whether the President agreed to this.

The President noted that he himself had included gravity bombs.

Gorbachev said those were details, and Shultz knew this.
The Soviet Union was proposing steps to meet U.S. concerns.
This included the SS-18, the heavy missiles, which would be
included in the 50% reductions too. Shultz was hearing this
for the first time. We should act to untie the knot. It can
be done. Otherwise Karpov and Kampelman will continue beating
around the bush. We need to take political decisions.

He proposed a 50% reduction in all types of these weapons,
Gorbachev repeated. Bombs and some other matters can be discussed
as we proceed. If the Soviets saw that the U.S. was not trying
to take side bypasses in order to gain some advantage, they
would take steps to accommodate us. If they saw us doing that,
they would say so.

- 9 -

The President replied that this should be taken up by the experts, if Gorbachev agreed to his proposal. He himself did not know all the numbers. But he did know that the Soviets outnumber us by a lot. If we cut by 50%, they would still have more than we do. Our number is smaller. But it was an interesting idea.

Gorbachev replied that this is not a matter for the experts. Passing over his data sheet, he said here is the data; let us cut this in half.

The President reminded Gorbachev he had said the idea was interesting. Gorbachev should give the U.S. side a chance. The Secretary commented that it was a bold idea, and we need bold ideas. Gorbachev agreed that this was what we need. Otherwise it goes back to Karpov and Kampelman. This was the kind of porridge we have eaten for years.

The President pointed out that the Soviet figures showed over 500 bombers for the U.S. In reality we had something over 200 functioning bombers. The rest were old and getting older. The Secretary suggested that those might be candidates for cutting. The idea was an interesting one, and we would look at it carefully.

The President asked if he could keep Gorbachev's data sheet. Gorbachev replied that he was giving it to the President. Now the President had all their secrets. Otherwise, he saw no way out of the forest. But if he felt the U.S. side was trying somehow to outsmart him, it would be the end of the negotiation.

The President said this would not happen. He asked if Gorbachev agreed to his proposal for a meeting of experts. Gorbachev said that he did, and would give the instructions.

Returning to the question of advantage, the President recalled the time, after the War, when we were the only ones to have nuclear weapons. We had offered to give them up, to turn them over to international control. We could have dictated to the whole world, but we didn't.

Gorbachev said he would like to turn to his next question. He saw that the U.S. did not like the U.S.-proposed zero option for medium-range missiles. The President replied that he liked it a lot, but on a global basis.

Gorbachev asked what had to be done for the global zero option to be acceptable. The President replied that if we got rid of them globally, this would be fine, and he was all for it.

- 10 -

But if they were eliminated only in Europe, and the Soviets retained a number of missiles supposedly targetted on Asiatic countries, but were in range of Europe and easily moved, we do not have equivalent systems. Zero should mean elimination of a whole category of weapons, for both Europe and Asia.

Gorbachev said that the U.S. had nuclear weapons in South Korea, on bases in Asia, and forward based systems there as well. He believed that U.S. concerns had been addressed: in Europe elimination of all medium-range missiles, a freeze on short-range missiles up to 1000 kilometers and then negotiations on them, and beginning negotiations to resolve the problem in Asia, and therefore the whole problem. The Soviets had set aside British and French systems. This was a concession. They had taken forward-based systems out. Why could the U.S. not take a single step to accommodate Soviet concerns, he asked. Their proposal was simple: resolve the issue in Europe, and begin negotiations to resolve it in Asia later.

The President said that we do not have ballistic missiles based in Asia. We have naval forces there, but both sides do, and the Soviet navy is bigger than ours.

Gorbachev replied that it does not matter to the Soviets if the bomb dropped on them is from a carrier or a base. The U.S. has bases in the Philippines. If the President was saying that these could be discussed, the Soviets were ready. All these questions should be discussed. On Europe, they should instruct their negotiators to agree to the full solution of complete elimination, setting aside the British and French systems, freezing short-range systems and then negotiating on them. In Asia both sides had concerns, but negotiations should begin, and he was sure the issues would be resolved.

The experts could discuss this in the evening, Gorbachev said.

The President agreed they should discuss it. He reminded Gorbachev that he had talked about these issues several times, including in Geneva. Gravity bombs should be distinguished from missiles which could blot out whole sections of the earth in minutes. A plane takes time to get to its target. That should not be compared to a missile which can get there in minutes. He was willing to talk about limiting the number of bombers both sides can have. But bombers cannot be compared to a missile.

Gorbachev asked what would happen if we eliminate the missiles and bombers with nuclear weapons are still flying. The President said this indicated the importance of not stopping here, with these weapons. We needed to tackle conventional weapons too. The other question is what if the Soviets had SS-20s in Asia and we took ours out of Europe. The Soviets could

- 11 -

then still reach targets in Europe. The deterrence is the threat
of retaliation. The Soviets still could hit. We have bombers,
but by the time they can drop the Soviets could already have
blown up Europe with their missiles. That was not much in the
way of retaliation. They would be facing extensive missile and
anti-aircraft defenses. That was not an equal approach.

The President said he kept forgetting Gorbachev was not
understanding before the interpretation.

Gorbachev replied that he did not think this was a logical
argumentation. They were suggesting solving the problem in
Europe first of all. They had compromised on the British and
French systems, but those would remain substantial arsenals.
Arithmetic is not enough. He thought the U.S. just didn't want
to remove its missiles from Europe. If that was so, the President
should just say so.

Soviet missiles in Asia could not reach targets in Europe,
unless that meant the Ukraine and Byelorussia.

Gorbachev said his question was: "If we find a solution
on Asian missiles, do you accept zero in Europe?"

The President said the answer was "Yes." We put our
missiles there because of the SS-20s. We had been requested
by our Allies to do so as a deterrence against a possible
attack by SS-20s. It had fallen to him to make the deployment;
the request had been made to the previous Administration. He
had seen maps that showed the SS-20s could hit, perhaps not
England, but France, Germany, countries in Central Europe, and
down to Greece and Turkey from Asian bases. Moreover they are
mobile, if the Soviets choose to move them.

The President asked whether it wasn't true that they
were revealing something he had talked about in Geneva. Before
we can get around to weapons we have to find out what causes
mistrust between us. If we could only get to that mistrust,
there would be no problem about what to do with the weapons.

Gorbachev replied that the President was right. He had
said Soviet missiles in Asia could not reach European targets.
All the experts know that. But the President did not believe
it. And in addition it was also true that any agreement would
be based on very clear criteria: no missile could be moved,
verification would be defined, and it would be strict verification.

Let our experts discuss medium-range missiles, Gorbachev
concluded, the President's ideas and his ideas. But did he
understand that if they reached solutions, the President favored

- 12 -

the zero option?

The President replied, "Yes."

Addressing the President, Gorbachev asked how, if what we are really doing is beginning to reduce strategic missiles and eliminate medium-range missiles, the two leaders of these nations could destroy the ABM Treaty, which is the only brake on very dangerous developments in a tense situation. How can we abandon it when we should be strengthening it, he asked. If we begin reductions, we should agree that it is important for both to have assurances that no one is going to develop systems that threaten stability and parity, especially when they are reducing.

Gorbachev continued that it is therefore logical that both sides proposed to accept the obligation not to withdraw from the treaty for a number of years. Numbers were the only difference. The Soviet side had proposed ten years, during which large-scale reductions would be taking place. This would certainly be needed. Otherwise one side could believe that the other was doing something behind its back. So it was logical to commit to 10 years and limit work to laboratory research only.

Turning to nuclear testing, Gorbachev said his proposal was a compromise which covered the U.S. proposal too. They would direct their negotiators to begin negotiations for a total ban, but this would take time, and in the first stage of negotiations a number of issues could be considered: reducing yields, the number of tests, the future of the treaties. All would be elements of these negotiations. Then no one could say we were engaging in cosmetic negotiations to deceive opinion. We would say we were beginning full-scope negotiations which would include all these things. It would be clear movement had begun toward a total ban, at some stage.

The President replied that this was interesting, and their people should take it up. With regard to the ABM Treaty, we believe the Soviets have violated it already by the extent of their defenses, what they have built. He himself thought that SDI was the greatest opportunity for peace of the 20th Century. But we are not proposing to annul the Treaty. Rather, we are proposing to add something to it with our proposals on defensive measures that both would have, and agreeing to share the benefits if these measures prove feasible.

Gorbachev proposed to arrange things as follows: he agreed to the President's proposal that experts meet at 8:00 PM to consider all the suggestions put forward in the two meetings between the President and the General Secretary. He would

- 13 -

be instructing his people to look for genuine solutions in all areas of nuclear arms, including verification. Now that we are getting down to the specifics, the Soviets would be fighting for verification. They will want it three times more than the U.S. side.

The President said we are both civilized countries, civilized people. When he was growing up -- a little before Gorbachev had been growing up -- there had been rules of warfare that protected non-combattants, civilians. Now, with the ABM Treaty, we have horrible missiles, whose principal victims are civilians. The only defense against them is the threat of slaughtering masses of other people. This is not civilized.

He was proposing something to change this, the President went on. It was something to be shared. It was not for one country only. It would protect people if a madman wanted to use such weapons -- take Qaddafi; if he had them he would certainly have used them. This would not happen in their time. It would be in someone else s time. But he asked Gorbachev to think about us two standing there and telling the world that we have this thing, and asking others to join us in getting rid of these terrible systems.

Gorbachev said his remarks in reply would be less philosophical, more prompted by the nature of what they had been discussing, which was practical.

The Soviets had proposed to enter a period of proceeding to reduce the nuclear weapons of both sides, both strategic and medium-range, and to strengthen the ABM Treaty so they could have the confidence needed while reducing. They think the period should be for a minimum of ten years, with very strict compliance with all the provisions of the ABM Treaty. That was his first point.

The second point, Gorbachev went on, was that they were accommodating the U.S. side concerning the continuation of laboratory research, to enable the U.S. to see whether it wanted a full-scope three-echelon strategic defense or something else. This, by the way, was consistent with Soviet plans too, for the U.S. would not be able to deploy the full system by then, but only some things in it. Within that period both countries would reach arsenals that, while still huge, would be much reduced. During that period anti-missile defense would make sure that no terrorist, or lunatic, or madman could do what he wanted.

Gorbachev continued that he could tell the President that at present SDI was not of military concern to the Soviet Union. The Soviet Union does not fear a three-echelon system if the U.S. decides that is what it wants. The Soviet response will be not symmetrical, but asymmetrical. The U.S. had money, and could do things the Soviets could not. The Soviets had a different concern.

- 14 -

It was to convince their people, and their allies, that they should be prepared to begin reductions while the ABM Treaty is being destroyed. This was not logical, and their people and allies would not understand it.

The President said that the ABM Treaty is a defensive systems treaty. The Soviets had built up quite a defense, and the U.S. had not. All the U.S. is saying is that in addition to the missiles covered by this treaty, here is something bigger, that we want the world to have. We are not building it for superiority. We want all to have it.' With the progress we are making we do not need 10 years. He could not have said that a few years ago, the President commented. We do not think it will take that long. Progress is being made.

Gorbachev said that the Soviets are not going to proceed with strategic defense themselves. They will have another approach. He took note of the President's statement that less than 10 years would be needed.

Let us turn our experts loose to work, Gorbachev said. The two of us have said a lot. Let them go to work now.

The President noted that they had been so wrapped up that they had not touched on regional, or bilateral or human rights issues, with a view to developing instructions to moving these along. He proposed that an experts' group meet on these issues too. On the U.S. side it would be Ridgway, Matlock, Rodman, Simons and Parris. He proposed that they go to work that night. Tomorrow would be the final day to see if we can come close on things.

Gorbachev agreed there should be two groups. He would think about the composition of the Soviet group, and Shevardnadze would get back to Shultz about it. Both should start at 8:00 PM.

The President proposed that the next morning's meeting be moved up to 10:00 AM. Gorbachev agreed.

The President said he had one closing remark. Gorbachev had said the Soviets do not need SDI, and have a better solution. Perhaps both sides should go ahead, and if the Soviets do better, they can give us theirs.

Gorbachev replied that the Soviet solution would not be better, but different. He was sorry to say that with regard to sharing he could not take the President seriously; speaking frankly. The U.S. was unwilling to give the Soviets oil drilling

- 15 -

equipment, automatic machinery, even milk factories. For the
U.S. to give the products of high technology would be a second
American Revolution, and it would not happen. It was better to
be realistic. This was more reliable.

The President said that if he thought the benefits would
not be given to others, he would give up the project himself.
Gorbachev rejoined that he did not think the President knew
what the project contained.

The President said he had some lists concerning human
rights to give Gorbachev. Gorbachev said he would accept
them, and, as always, they would be carefully considered.

Drafted:TWSimons, Jr.
10/11/86

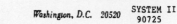

United States Department of State

Washington, D.C. 20520   SYSTEM II
90725

SECRET/SENSITIVE

MEMORANDUM OF CONVERSATION

Date: Sunday, October 12, 1986
Time: 10:00 am - 1:35 pm
Place   Hofdi House, Reykjavik

Participants

US Side   Soviet Side

The President   The General Secretary
Secretary Shultz   Foreign Minister Shevardnadze
Mr. Parris   Mr. Uspenskiy
Mr. Zarechnak (Interpreter)   Mr. Paleschenky (Interpreter)

Gorbachev opened the discussion with a quip: the Bible said that first had come the first day, then the second, etc. The two leaders were now on their second day; there was still a long way before the seventh. The President said that the two should be resting. Gorbachev agreed, as it was Sunday.

Gorbachev suggested that the session begin with a review of the progress achieved by the two groups which had met throughout the night before on arms control and non-arms control issues. After Gorbachev declined the opportunity to speak first, the President gave his assessment.

The President said that, with a few exceptions, he was disappointed with what had been achieved by the arms control group. With respect to START, the President understood that the sides were able to come to substantial agreement -- with give and take on both sides. Of course, there had been substantial work in this area, which had developed a sizeable amount of common ground. It was the President's understanding that the working group had been able to agree on a formulation for the outlines of a 50% reduction of strategic arsenals that should move the negotiations substantially ahead. Both sides should be proud of this achievement.

On INF, the President understood that the sides had discussed a number of issues, including SRINF, the duration of an interim agreement, and verification, and that they had come to the conclusion that these issues could be handled in negotiations. But the group had not been able to solve the issue of reductions of LRINF missles in Asia. The last issue

SECRET/SENSITIVE
DECL: OADR

DECLASSIFIED
NLS *E97-004 #14*
BY ____ NARA, DATE *1/14/00*

- 2 -

had been discussed at great length. The question was now
fairly simple, not technical at all. We had made clear since
the time of our initial zero-zero proposal -- a proposal to
eliminate all of the class of LRINF missiles, worldwide --
that we required a global agreement. This was thus not a new
issue for us. It was an issue that we could no longer ignore
if we were to make progress. The President said he could not
and would not accept a situation in which sizeable reductions
in Europe, even to zero, were not matched by proportional
redutions in Asia. The Soviets knew the reasons for this --
the mobility of the SS-20 and the impact such a shift in the
balance of SS-20's to Asia would have on our Asian allies.
These were not new arguments. However, they were real
concerns to the President. Our allies in both Europe and Asia
fully supported this position. Our allies in both Europe and
Asia fully supported this position, in fact they insisted upon
it for their own security.

The President reminded Gorbachev that, in his most recent
letter, Gorbachev had written that, with regard to Soviet
systems in Asia, "a mutually acceptable formula can be found
and I am ready to propose one, provided there is a certainty
that a willingness can be found to resolve the issue of medium
range missiles in Europe does exist." This issue, the
President continued, must be dealt with on a global basis.
The President had felt he and Gorbachev had agreed to pursue
an interim, global agreement. They had agreed on an interim
INF agreement, with equal ceilings on U.S. and Soviet LRINF
warheads on each side of Europe, and an equal ceiling on U.S.
and Soviet LRINF missiles worldwide. We could accept the
Soviet idea of 100 in Europe, if other elements could be
worked out. The Soviets had proposed 100 warheads on each
side in Europe. If agreement were reached on other aspects of
an interim agreement, we would have no problem with that
number

The U.S. had long called for proportional reductions in
Asia. If we reduced to 100 warheads in Europe, and reduced
Asian systems in the same proportion, the Asian ceiling would
come out to something like 63. 100 in Europe/100 in Asia was
acceptable. In the right context, we could accept 100 in
Europe and 100 in Asia. The President suggested he and
Gorbachev settle now on 100/100 and instruct our negotiators
to work out details.

Gorbachev interrupted briefly to clarify that the
President's proposal was for 100 LRINF warheads each for the
U.S. and Soviet Union in Europe and an additional 100 for the
Soviet Union in Asia. The President explained that the U.S.,
under its proposal, would also have the right to deploy an

- 3 -

additional 100 warheads on a global basis. In response to a
question, the President confirmed that those 100 would be
based on U.S. territory.

On defense and space, the President felt he and Gorbachev
recognized the basic differences in the two sides'
approaches. For his part, the President recognized that
Gorbachev at this point was not prepared to agree with him;
but the President was not prepared to move from the course
that he believed correct. Recognizing this, the President
proposed that he and Gorbachev instruct their negotiators to
focus on what the President felt to be three critical issues.
Of the three, the U.S. believed that only the first two
deserved immediate attention, but recognized Soviet concerns
about the third and included it to respond to those concerns.
The questions were:

-- First, how could activities with respect to the
investigation of strategic defenses be synchronized with our
shared goals of eliminating ballistic missiles?

-- Second, what should the conditions and timeframe be for
increased reliance on strategic defenses?

-- Third, until these conditions are met, what common
understanding might be reached on activities under the ABM
Treaty on advanced strategic defenses?

At a minimum, the President asked, could the two sides not
agree to instruct our negotiators to address these three
questions in the hope of using them to move our positions
closer together?

Moving to the question of nuclear testing, the President
said that here, too, he had been disappointed with the outcome
of the previous evening's efforts. He could only hope that
that outcome had reflected a simple lack of imagination on the
part of one or the other side's representatives.

The President noted that there was agreement in principle
on the fact of immediate negotiations, on the agenda, on the
order of subjects, and on the ultimate outcome. The President
understood, however, that the sides could not get agreement
because of an argument on how these negotiations should be
characterized. He proposed that the two sides simply record
that they agreed to immediate negotiations on testing issues.
We were prepared to note that the ultimate objective, which we
believed could be reached in association with the elimination
of all nuclear weapons, was the cessation of all testing.

- 4 -

We both agreed that the first order of business should be
the resolution of the remaining verification issues associated
with existing treaties. With this agreement, it was possible
to get started and characterize the negotiations in a way
which met both sides' needs. But we had to agree on agenda
and priority. Was it not possible for the two leaders to
instruct their ministers to sort out the language quickly and
record this agreement in suitable fashion.

In response to a question by Gorbachev as to what language
the U.S. proposed with respect to testing, the President read
from a paper prepared by the U.S. arms control working group
the night before.

"The U.S. and Soviet Union will begin negotiations on
nuclear testing. The agenda for these negotiations will first
be to resolve remaining verification issues associated with
existing treaties. With this resolved, the U.S. and U.S.S.R.
will immediately proceed, in parallel with the reduction and
elimination of nuclear weapons, to address further
step-by-step limitations on testing, leading ultimately to the
elimination of nuclear testing."

Gorbachev indicated that the U.S. position was not clear
to him.

Turning to the work of the second working group, which had
addressed non-arms control matters, the President said that
its participants had done a fine job. Their breakthrough on
nuclear fusion was particularly commendable.

Gorbachev asked to give an initial reaction to the
President's presentation, and to ask a few questions regarding
the points the President had covered .

Referring to the President's expression of disappointment
with the results of the arms control working group, despite
the fact that it had labored for ten hours, Gorbachev said he
had also been very disappointed. The Soviets felt the
proposals they had brought to Reykjavik had been highly
constructive in spirit -- and not just in philosophical
terms. They had made real concessions to the U.S in a number
of negotiations and had sought to establish conditions for
reducing and eliminating nuclear weapons. But they had found
that, instead of seeking as they had to give an impulse to the
discussions, the U.S. was trying to drag things backward.

- 5 -

As Gorbachev had said previously, the Geneva negotiations prior to the current meeting had reached an impasse. New approaches were needed, as were political will and an ability to think in broad terms, to escape this dead-end. The Soviets had crafted their proposals with this in mind. They had expected the same from the Americans.

It was possible to record some areas of agreement, e.g., with respect to strategic systems. Both sides had agreed to reduce by 50% all components in this category, both as to warheads and delivery vehicles.

INF was an issue over which the two sies had struggled for a long time. The problems were particularly difficult because they involved not just the two countries directly concerned, but their respective allies as well. The Soviets felt that their current position satisfied all U.S. concerns: Moscow had agreed to put aside consideration of UK/French systems; it had agreed that the problem of shorter range systems existed, and had agreed to freeze and to enter into negotiations on such systems. As for Asian systems, they bore no relation to the problem of reducing INF in Europe. Nonetheless, as the U.S. had insisted on linking European systems with those in Asia, the Soviets were willing to take Asian systems in to account.

Gorbachev said he had developed the impression that the President and his administration's approach to arms control proceeded from the false impression that the Soviet Union was more interested in nuclear disarmament than the U.S. Perhaps the U.S. felt it could use such leverage to force the Soviet Union to capitulate in certain areas. This was a dangerous illusion. Such a scenario could never occur.

The President had mentioned the possibility of an interim INF agreement, Gorbachev continued. The Soviet Union could not accept such an interim solution. It was not interested in palliatives or make-shift solutions. But if the question of Asian systems could be resolved -- not just put into the negotiations, but dealt with in specific terms -- the U.S. could agree to zero systems in Europe and some sort of equal number in Asia. Was this a correct understanding of the American position?

The President described the U.S. view of the problem posed by Soviet SS-20's. As these weapons were mobile, they could be viewed as in two categories (i.e. for use in either Asia or Europe). If the Soviets were left with 100 systems in Asia after the U.S. had withdrawn its own LRINF deterrent from

- 6 -

Europe, the Soviets would gain an enormous advantage. This
would pose great difficulties for U.S. relations with its
friends in Europe, countries with which the Soviet Union was
also seeking to improve relations. In response to Gorbachev's
interruption that it was clear nothing would come of this
discussion, the President invited the General Secretary to
make some suggestions of his own.

Gorbachev complained that the President appeared to have
forgotten that the Soviets had already agreed to leave out
UK/French systems -- a major concern. How, Gorbachev asked,
could the President speak of a zero solution in Europe when
the Soviets would be obliged to eliminate their INF, while
U.S. allies would retain their nuclear forces. Even though
American allies were integrated into a common military
structure, the Soviets were prepared not to count these
systems in order to reach an INF agreement. With respect to
the possibility that Soviet systems in Asia could be moved
westward, the subject should not even be discussed at the
President's and Gorbachev's level. Any agreement to include
Asian systems would be verifiable: if there were a single fact
of Asian systems being redeployed, it could be made to nullify
the agreement. Thus, the concerns the President had raised
were not serious. If he did not want an agreement, he should
say so. Otherwise, neither leader should waste his time.

The President said we did not see UK and French nuclear
weapons as part of NATO. The governments of those countries
had made clear their deterrents were for their own defense.
If the FRG, for example, were attacked, these systems would
not be used. In any case, Soviet central systems were an
adequate counter to such systems.

Gorbachev inquired why, given the concern the President
had expressed about the FRG, the Soviets should be any less
concerned about the defense of the GDR or other Warsaw Pact
allies. As for UK systems, when Gorbachev had been in
Britain, he had recalled to Mrs. Thatcher a published letter
from her to SACEUR. The letter had expressed gratitude for
U.S. assistance in modernizing the British nuclear deterrent,
and had noted pointedly that these modernized forces would
make the Soviets sit up and take notice. Gorbachev had
explained to her that this was precisely what he had done, so
she had no reason to be displeased.

More seriously, he continued, the two leaders were not at
a press conference. They both knew the facts, so there was no
reason to speak in banalities. The Soviets knew what the
situation was with respect to the integration of UK forces;
they even knew how targetting had been integrated. The

- 7 -

importance of the topic the two leaders were discussing made
it necessary that they speak frankly.

The President pointed out that, in fact, the Soviet Union
and United States were the only two real nuclear powers.
Other countries having nuclear weapons had them basically in a
defensive mode. The President envisioned that, if the U.S.
and Soviet Union were to start the process of reducing their
own nuclear forces to zero, and would stand shoulder-to-
shoulder in telling other nations that they must eliminate
their own nuclear weapons, it would be hard to think of a
country that would not do so.

Gorbachev agreed. He felt, in fact, that the present
chance might be the only one in this respect. Gorbachev had
not not been in a position a year ago, to say nothing of two
or three years ago, to make the kind of proposals he was-not
making. He might not be able to make the same proposals in a
year or so. Time passed; things changed. Reykjavik would be
simply a memory.

The President remarked that the two were in the same
situation in this respect. But if one were soon to be without
authority, it was all the more important to use the time
available to contribute something to the world -- to free the
world from the nuclear threat.

Gorbachev said that the proposals he had brought to
Reykjavik left his own conscience clear. He could look the
President in the eye and say that, it if were impossible to
reach agreements, it was all right. But the situation in
Geneva had been marking time, and no agreements had been in
sight. Now the U.S. did not appear to feel obliged to take
Soviet concerns into account, while the Soviets had met
American concerns. Could the two leaders not agree as
follows: U.S. and Soviet INF would be eliminated from Europe;
UK/French systems would be left aside; there would be a freeze
and subsequent negotiations on short range systems; and the
Soviets would be willing to find a solution to the problem of
Asian systems.

In response to the President's invitation to describe in
greater detail what the Soviets had in mind for Asian systems,
Gorbachev elaborated on the proposals he had just made. U.S.
and Soviet systems would be eliminated from Europe. UK/French
systems would not be counted. There would be a freeze and
subsequent negotiations on shorter range systems. In Asia,
the Soviets would accept the U.S. formula that there be 100
warheads on Soviet systems, and the U.S 100 warheads on its
territory. The Soviets would accept this even though it would

- 8 -

require time to reduce several times, by an order of magnitude
that Gorbachev could not even compute. As the U.S. insisted
on posing <u>ultimata</u> and as the President was unwilling to make
proposals of his own, the Soviet Union would accept this.
After a prompt from <u>Shevardnadze</u>, <u>Gorbachev</u> added that this
concession would be made despite the U.S. build-up in the
Pacific basin. This should show how serious the Soviet Union
was to reach agreements.

The <u>President</u> said he agreed to the proposal Gorbachev had
described.

<u>Gorbachev</u> said that was good. He then asked when the U.S.
would start making concessions of its own. The two leaders
had gone through half the agenda and there had been no
movement from the U.S side. The next issue would be the test
of the U.S.'s readiness to meet the Soviets half way.

Prefacing his remarks on the ABM Treaty, Gorbachev
recalled that the two sides had agreed in principle to reduce
strategic forces by 50%. Agreement had also been reached on
eliminating LRINF from Europe; on freezing and subsequently
starting up negotiations on shorter range INF; and on 100
Soviet warheads in Asia, with the U.S. to have the right to
the same number on its territory. These were unprecedented
steps. They required responsible further steps in the
implementation phase. This raised the question of
verification, an issue which now became acute. The U.S. would
find that the Soviets would be more vigorous than the U.S. in
insisting on stringent verification requirements as the two
countries entered the stage of effective disarmament. If it
proved impossible to agree on such provisions, it would be
impossible to reduce strategic and intermediate range weapons.

With respect to the ABM Treaty, Gorbachev expressed his
conviction that nothing should be allowed to "shake" the ABM
regime or confidence in an ABM Treaty of unlimited duration as
deep reductions began to be implemented in strategic weapons.
Gorbachev felt the President could agree to this proposition.
As Gorbachev had said the day before, but would repeat, once
one decided to reduce nuclear arms, one had to be certain that
one side could not act behind the back of the other. So it
was necessary to strengthen the ABM regime. The Soviet
proposal for a ten year commitment not to withdraw from the
Treaty would be a step forward toward strengthening the ABM
regime.

In preparing their position, the Soviets had taken into
account the President's attachment to the SDI program. Thus,
uner the ten-year pledge, SDI-related research in laboratories

- 9 -

would not be banned. This was not a strict limitation on
SDI. The Soviets knew where the program stood. The U.S. had
scored breakthroughs in one or two areas. Moscow knew which
they were. But ten years would enable the two sides to solve
the problems of reducing nuclear weapons, and so was
necessary. The type of arrangement he was proposing,
Gorbachev reiterated, would pose neither political, practical
nor technical impediments to the President's program.

The President replied that the U.S. had no intention of
violating the ABM Treaty. It had never done so, even though,
as the Soviets knew, it believed the Soviet Union had itself
done more than was permitted by the Treaty.

With respect the SDI, the President recalled that he had
made a pledge to the American people that SDI would contribute
to disarmament and peace, and not be an offensive weapon. He
could not retreat from that pledge. The U.S. had proposed a
binding Treaty which would provide for the sharing of research
which demonstrated a potential for defensive applications.
This would facilitate the elimination of nuclear weapons. The
President repeated that he could not retreat from his pledge.
We would share the fruits of our research -- and out of our
own self-interest. If everyone had access to the relevant
technology, it would be a threat to no one. The President did
not see why SDI could not be made a part of the ABM Treaty.
He was dedicated to the establishment of mutual defenses
against nuclear weapons. Reaffirming once more that he could
not retreat, the President noted that Secretary Shultz wished
to make a point.

The Secretary observed that both the President and General
Secretary had spoken in terms of eliminating nuclear weapons.
In what Gorbachev had said a moment before, the Secretary
thought he had heard something a little different. He wanted
to be sure he had heard correctly. Gorbachev had seemed to
link his 10 year no-withdrawal pledge to the length of time
necessary to eliminate nuclear weapons. Was that in fact the
link that the General Secretary had in mind? Would the
schedule be linked to what he would be doing on START and INF,
so that, at the end of the ten years of which Gorbachev had
spoken there would be no ballistic missiles, to set aside
other nuclear weapons?

Gorbachev reaffirmed that this was the case. The proposal
he had made last January had called for 50% reductions in
strategic forces and elimination of INF in the first phase of
a process aimed at eliminating all nuclear weapons.
Subsequent stages would involve further reductions, including
reductions by third countries. But major reductions by the

- 10 -

U.S. and U.S.S.R. would take place in this period, and so the
ten year period Gorbachev had mentioned was of decisive
importance. He was not retreating from, but reinforcing, the
proposals he had made earlier. If one were serious about
reducing nuclear weapons, therefore, there was a need to
reinforce the ABM regime. Gorbachev could not agree to
anything which would weaken the ABM Treaty. His goal was to
strengthen the Treaty, not revise it as the U.S. had
proposed. There was no logic to such an approach. Were the
Soviet Union to accept it, the world would conclude it was
doing so purely out of egotistical self-interest. Gorbachev
would be unable to go before the Soviet people or the world
with such a proposal. That was why the 10-year commitment he
was seeking was necessary if there were to be major reductions
in offensive forces.

Research was a different matter. The Soviets had taken
into account the President's concerns. They knew he was bound
by the pledge he had made to his own people and to the world.
Research would continue, and this would show that SDI was
alive. But such work should not go beyond the framework of
laboratory research. There could be testing, even mock-up in
laboratories. And such efforts would ensure against the
appearance of a nuclear madman of the type the President had
often mentioned.

The President countered that in fact it would not. What
the Hell, he asked, was it that we were defending? The ABM
Treaty said that we could not defend ourselves except by means
of the 100 ground based systems which we have never deployed.
If said our only defense is that, if someone wants to blow us
up, the other will retaliate. Such a regime did not give
protection; it limited protection. Why the Hell should the
world have to live for another ten years under the threat of
nuclear weapons if we have decided to eliminate them? The
President failed to see the magic of the ABM regime, whose
only assurance of safety was the doctrine of Mutual Assured
Destruction. It would be better to eliminate missiles so that
our populations could sleep in peace. At the same time, the
two leaders could give the world a means of protection that
would put the nuclear genie back in his bottle. The next
generation would reap the benefits when the President and
General Secretary were no longer around.

Gorbachev recalled for the President what he described as
the long and complicated history of the ABM Treaty. It had
not come as a bolt from the blue but after years of discussion
by responsible leaders, who ultimately recognized the
impossibility of creating an ABM system, and who concluded
that, if the attempt were made, it would only fuel the arms

- 11 -

race and make it impossible to reduce nuclear arms. No one
in the Soviet leadership, nor he personally, could agree to
steps which would undercut the Treaty. So on this point it
appeared the two leaders would have to report that they had
opposite views.

The next item, Gorbachev felt, should be negotiations on a
comprehensive test ban. When the Soviets had pulled together
their current position, they had worked from U.S. proposals to
try to see how the two sides' approaches coincided. What was
their line of thinking? The two leaders should direct their
representatives to start negotiations on ending nuclear
testing.

The talks would proceed for a certain period of time.
During that period, each side could do what it liked, i.e.,
tests would be permitted. To take into account U.S concerns,
the Soviets were prepared to agree that the agenda for such a
first phase could include: test yields, the number of tests,
the Threshold Test Ban and Peaceful Nuclear Explosions
Treaties (TTBT/PNET), and verification.

These were all U.S. issues which the Soviets had
incorporated into their approach. In contrast, Gorbachev
sensed from what the President had said that the U.S. was only
considering its own interests. Specifically, U.S. proposals
did not adequately deal with the problem of a comprehensive
test ban. Gorbachev could not agree to a proposal which
reflected only American interests.

The conversation, he continued, had reached a point where
it was time for the American side to make a move in the Soviet
direction on the ABM Treaty and CTB. There was a need for the
flexibility which would demonstrate whether the U.S. was in
fact interested in finding mutually acceptable solutions to
problems. Gorbachev had heard it said that the President did
not like to make concessions. But he also recalled an
American expression which seemed apt: "it takes two to
tango." With respect to the major questions of arms control
and nuclear disarmament, the two leaders were the only
partners in sight. Was the President prepared to dance?

The President in response sought to put the U.S. position
on testing in an historical perspective. For three years,
during the late fifties, there had been a moratorium on
nuclear tests. Then the Soviet Union had broken the
moratorium with a series of tests unprecedented in their
number and scope. U.S. experts had subsequently determined
that the Soviet Union had been preparing for that test series
throughout the period of the moratorium. President Kennedy

had resumed testing, but because we had made no preparations
to test during the moratorium period, we were placed at a
severe disadvantage. President Kennedy had vowed we would
never again be caught unprepared in this area. But in fact we
were still behind. The Soviets had largely completed the
modernization of their weapons stockpile before announcing
their moratorium.

In any case, a comprehensive test ban would have to follow
reductions in nuclear weapons. And there must also be
adequate verification. Until now, the Soviets had been
unwilling to address this issue seriously. Now that they had
done so, the U.S. stood prepared to join them. But, in view
of the historical precedents he had mentioned, the President
felt Gorbachev would understand why, to quote another
Americanism, we were "once burned, twice shy." Nonetheless,
the U.S. had made concessions to Soviet concerns. The
President again read the language on testing developed the
night before by the U.S. working group, highlighting the
statement's final sentence on a comprehensive test ban as an
ultimate goal of negotiations.

Gorbachev indicated that the U.S. language was not
acceptable to the Soviet side. In their own package, the
Soviets had proposed that representatives be instructed to
start negotiations on "banning nuclear testing." In an
initial phase, these talks could deal with other issues. But
the final goal must be to achieve a CTB on both military and
civilian tests. Shevardnadze interjected that the ultimate
goal should be stated first. In response to the President's
remark that the U.S. language covered the concern Gorbachev
had expressed, Gorbachev complained that the U.S formulation
suggested that it did not want to state directly the subject
and goal of the negotiations. Instead, it appeared the U.S.
wanted the talks to drag on forever. Under the U.S. formula,
talks could go well beyond the ten years during which it would
be necessary to find a solution to the problem of nuclear
weapons. The Soviet Union would not help provide the U.S. a
free hand to test as much and as long as it wanted.
Shevardnadze remarked that acceptance of the U.S. formulation
would call into question the ultimate goal of reducing and
ultimately eliminating nuclear weapons.

The President said that perhaps there was some difficulty
in the translation, but it appeared to him that the U.S.
language met Soviet concerns. (Gorbachev quipped that
Zarechnak could tell the President that were were indeed
talking about totally different things.) The President asked
Gorbachev if the U.S. formulation would be more acceptable if
the final sentence were moved to the front of the paragraph.

- 13 -

Gorbachev replied that it would not. Perhaps, he suggested, Shultz and Shevardnadze should be tasked with working out a formula. The problem, he said, was that the U.S. was saying that there could be talks -- talks identified as having the "ultimate objective" of a CTB -- but focused primarily on other things. Work on a CTB would start only at a later stage. But we should make it clear that we had already "started" work in that area. What was needed were clear-cut formulae without side-tracks. What the Soviets were proposing, Gorbachev recapitulated, was talks on a CTB, during which testing could continue, and in the first stage of which ancillary issues such as verification could be dealt with. In a second stage of the same talks, there would be movement toward a complete ban on nuclear tests. As a lawyer, Gorbachev felt confident that such an arrangement would allow no room for side-tracking.

The President remarked that Gorbachev had touched on something very basic with respect to our problem with one another. Gorbachev's remarks reflected a belief that the U.S. was in some way trying to attain an advantage out of hostility toward the Soviet Union. While it would do no good to tell Gorbachev he was wrong, since it would only be the President's word (which the President knew to be true), the President could say that we harbored no hostile intentions toward the Soviets. We recognized the differences in our two systems. But the President felt that we could live as friendly competitors. Each side mistrusted the other. But, the President affirmed, the evidence was all on our side.

To illustrate his point, the President began a quote from Marx, prompting Gorbachev to observe jocularly that the President had dropped Lenin for Marx. The President countered that Marx had said first much of what Lenin said later. In any case, both had expressed the view that socialism had to be global in scope to succeed. The only mortality was that which advanced socialism. And it was a fact that every Soviet leader but Gorbachev -- at least so far -- had endorsed in speeches to Soviet Communist Party Congresses the objective of establishing a world communist state.

Moreover, even when the two countries had been allies during World War II, Soviet suspicions had been such that Moscow had resisted U.S. shuttle bombing missions to and from Soviet territory. After the war, the U.S. had proposed on nineteen separate occasions -- at a time when it had a monopoly on nuclear weapons -- the elimination of such weapons. The Soviet Union had not only rebuffed such offers, but had placed nuclear missiles in Cuba in the sixties. The

- 14 -

President could go on, but he wanted simply to make the point
that such behavior revealed a belief on the Soviets' part in a
world wide mission which gave us legitimate grounds to suspect
Soviet motives. The Soviets had no grounds for believing that
the U.S. wanted war. When Gorbachev came to the United
States, he would see that the last thing the American people
wanted was to exchange their life-styles for war. The
President suspected the same was true for the average Soviet
citizen.

Gorbachev observed that, with respect to Marx and Lenin,
history was full of examples of those who had sought to
overcome their philosophy by force. All had failed.
Gorbachev would advise the President not to waste time and
energy to such an end.

But to return to the present, and, Gorbachev noted,
because the President had initiated "invitation" comments in
this vein, Gorbachev felt obliged to say that the Soviet Union
recognized the right of the U.S. people to their own values,
beliefs, society. There were things Soviets liked about the
U.S. and things they did not. But they recognized the
Americans were a great people who had a right to conduct their
affairs as they saw fit. It was up to the American people to
choose their government and their President. Thus Gorbachev
had been surprised when he had heard of a recent statement by
the President to the effect that the President remained true
to the principles of his 1981 Westminister speech. That
speech had referred to the Soviet Union as an evil empire; it
had called for a crusade against socialism in order to
relegate it to the ash heap of history. What would the
outcome be if the U.S. sought to act according to these
principles? Would we fight one another? Gorbachev failed to
understand how such a statement could be considered an
appropriate "forward" to the Reykjavik meeting. In any case,
he reminded the President, the President had initiated the
discussion.

The President reminded Gorbachev in turn that there was a
Communist party in the United States. Its members could and
did organize and run for public office. They were free to try
to persuade the people of the validity of their philosophy.
That was not true in the Soviet Union. The Soviets enforced
rather than persuaded. Similarly, when communist parties took
power in third world countries, they quickly eliminated other
parties by force. In the U.S., anyone could organize his own
party. There was only one party in the Soviet Union, and a
majority of the Soviet population were excluded from
membership. So there was a fundamental difference in the two
societies' approaches: the U.S. believed that people should
have the right to determine their own form of government.

- 15 -

Gorbachev indicated that he would be happy to have a
wide-ranging conversation with the President on the moral,
philosophical and ethical issues raised by the President's
remarks. For the moment, he would simply note that the
situation in the Soviet Union was not as the President had
described it, and that the President's remarks showed that
they differed fundamentally in their basic conceptions of the
world. But the two leaders seemed to agree that each side had
the right to organize its society according to its own
philosophical or religious beliefs. This was an issue which
the two might come back to at another time. Gorbachev had no
desire to quarrel. He was convinced, in fact, that, while he
and the President might have different characters and
conceptions, a man-to-man relationship between them was
possible. The President said he looked forward to welcoming
Gorbachev at some point as a new member of the Republican
Party. Gorbachev commented that there had been a profusion of
parties in Russia both before and after the Revolution. These
things were the result of historical processes. He commented
that Secretary Shultz appeared to have a contribution to make.

The Secretary observed that it appeared there was the
beginning of a joint statement on strategic weapons.
(Gorbachev nodded.) On the basis of the two leaders'
discussion, it should also be possible to formulate a similar
statement on INF. (Gorbachev again nodded.) On
Space/ABM/SDI, there had been no agreement, but the two sides
had identified and characterized their areas of disagreement.
These appeared not to deal with the question of whether or not
to adhere to the ABM Treaty, since the U.S. was adhering, but
rather over the period involved.

Gorbachev commented that, in the context of what had been
agreed to on strategic and intermediate range offensive arms,
a statement on adherence to the ABM Treaty would be
necessary. That was obvious.

Shevardnadze asked if the approach outlined in the
President's letter to the question of the period of
non-withdrawal from the ABM Treaty remained valid. The
Secretary reminded Shevardnadze that the President had called
for a two-stage approach. That was still on the table.
Gorbachev asked if that meant the U.S. did not accept a ten
year period.

The Secretary suggested three points to describe where the
two sides were. They could be cast in terms of the leaders'
having instructed their negotiators to explore the following
areas to bridge existing differences. The Secretary then

- 16 -

read the three questions the President had read in his opening presentation.

When the Secretary reached the second point, on a "cooperative transition to advanced strategic defenses", Gorbachev interrupted to point out that the Soviets did not recognize the concept. It was the U.S which intended to deploy SDI. The Soviets would not make such an arrangement possible. Their concept was different. The Secretary continued to read the three points, noting that the final point was designed to respond to Soviet concerns.

The President, the Secretary continued, had made clear he would not give up SDI. Gorbachev had said he recognized that to be the President's position, and that the Soviets had made an effort to accommodate it. Gorbachev nodded, adding with a laugh that some even felt he was trying to encourage development of SDI so as to increase the U.S. defense burden. Thus, as it turned out, he was on the President's side, and the President had not even known it.

The President noted that, as the oldest person in the room, he was the only one who could remember how, after World War I, poison gas had been outlawed. But people kept their gas masks. And it was a good thing, because poison gas came back. The same could happen with nuclear weapons: if, after their elimination, someone were to bring them back, we would need something to deal with that.

Gorbachev commented that the preceding conversation had convinced him of the veracity of reports that the President did not like to make concessions. The President clearly did not want to give any concessions on the question of the ABM Treaty -- its duration and strength, or on the cessation of nuclear testing.

The President replied that he felt we had agreed on testing.

Shevardnadze asked if it would be possible to consider the period during which there would be no withdrawal from the ABM Treaty. It might be possible to reach agreement on this point. Gorbachev reiterated that a much more rigid adherence to the ABM Treaty, for a specific period of time -- say, ten years -- would be necessary to create the confidence necessary to proceed with deep cuts in offensive sytems. Returning to the Secretary's earlier point, he underscored that the ten year period would coincide with the most significant reductions on the offensive side. Shevardnadze pointed out that there was a question of principle: if the two sides

- 17 -

could not agree on a period for non-withdrawal from the ABM
Treaty, it would be impossible to agree on reductions.
Gorbachev added that the Soviets had proposed a package, and
that individual elements of their proposals must be regarded
as a package.

The President expressed the view that there should be no
such linkage. The U.S., for its part, believed the Soviet
Union already to be in violation of the ABM Treaty. The U.S.
had not even built systems provided for in the Treaty.

Gorbachev interrupted to note that, on the first two
questions (START and INF) it would be possible to say there
were common points. On the second (ABM and testing), there
had been a meaningful exchange of views, but no common points.

With that, the meeting could end. It had not been in
vain. But it had not produced the results that had been
expected in the Soviet Union, and that Gorbachev personally
had expected. Probably the same could be said for the United
States. One had to realisitic. In political life one had to
follow reality. The reality today was that it was possible to
reach agreements on some major, interrelated questions. But
because there was a lack of clarity, the connection had been
disrupted. So the two sides remained where they had been
before Reykjavik.

Gorbachev said the President would now report to
Congress. Gorbachev would make his report to the Politburo
and the Supreme Soviet. The process would not stop.
Relations would continue. For his part, Gorbachev was sorry
he and the President had failed to provide a new impulse for
arms control and disarmament. This was unfortunate, and
Gorbachev regretted it .

The President said he did, too. He had thought we had
agreements on 50% reductions, on INF, on considering what to
do about the ABM Treaty, and on reducing nuclear testing. Was
this not so? Were the two leaders truly to depart with
nothing?

Gorbachev said that that was the case. He suggested the
two devote a few minutes to humanitarian and regional
questions, which, he pointed out, had been discussed by the
second (non-arms control) working group. The President
agreed, and the two briefly reviewed papers prepared by the
working group the night before.

The President asked to make a few comments on human
rights. He had no intention of saying publicly that he had
demanded anything from Gorbachev in terms of such issues as
family reunification and religious persecution. But he did

- 18 -

want to urge Gorbachev to move forward in this area, since it
was a major factor domestically in limiting how far the
President could go in cooperation with the Soviet Union. As
he had told Gorbachev before, one in every eight people in the
United States had family connections of some sort to the
Soviet Union, so a significant part of the American population
was concerned by such phenomena as the shut-down in emigration
from the Soviet Union. We would continue to provide lists of
people we had reason to believe wanted to depart. And if the
Soviets loosened up, we would not exploit it. We would simply
express our appreciation.

Gorbachev expressed regret that there was not more time to
address humanitarian questions. There were some specific
concerns he had wanted to put before the President. And he
wanted to make clear that Soviet public opinion was also
concerned about the state of human rights in the United States.

One question he did want to broach had to do with
expanding the flow of information between the two countries.
This was of potentially great importance. On the U.S. side,
the Voice of America over the years had developed an enormous
capability of broadcasting to the Soviet Union. It broadcast
round the clock, in many languages, from many transmitters
outside the Soviet Union. The Soviets did not have the same
opportunity for their broadcasts to be heard in the United
States, and so, to put things on an equal basis, they jammed
VOA broadcasts.

What Gorbachev proposed was this: the Soviets would stop
jamming VOA if the U.S. would help the Soviet Union enhance
its ability to broadcast to the United States. Perhaps the
U.S. could help the Soviets rent a radio station for this
purpose, or intervene with some of its neighbors to facilitate
the establishment of Soviet transmitters close to the U.S. In
this way, both sides would be able to relay their points of
view to the others' population.

The President pointed out that, in the U.S., we recognized
the right of the individual to hear all points of view. The
press conference Gorbachev would give after their meeting
would be carried by the U.S. media. The same would not happen
in the Soviet Union. In response to Gorbachev's request for
an answer to his specific proposal, the President agreed to
look into the matter on his return to Washington, and said he
would be supportive.

Picking up on the President's remarks on the media,
Gorbachev pointed out that half of the foreign films shown in
the Soviet Union were American. Virtually no Soviet films

- 19 -

were shown in the U.S. There was no equality in this
arrangement.

The President replied that this was a function of the
market, rather than any attempt to ban Soviet films.
(Gorbachev commented that the President was trying to avoid a
direct answer.) The U.S. government could not dictate what
films private entrepreneurs showed. The President noted that
he did not know now films were distributed in the Soviet
Union, even though he used to make films. Gorbachev said that
here was a paradox: in an allegedly democratic country there
are obstacles to Soviet films; in an allegedly non-democratic
country half the foreign films were American. This did not
tally with the view of Soviet society the President had
described earlier.

The President saw the explanation to the paradox in the
differences between private and government ownership. In the
Soviet Union, there was no free enterprise. In the U.S.,
films were distributed by private industry. If the Soviet
Union wanted to, it could do what other countries had done and
form its own distributing company. If it could convince local
theatres to show its films, fine. But the government could
not order them to.

Raising another question, Gorbachev asked why recent
tele-bridges between cities in the U.S. and U.S.S.R. had not
been shown at all in the U.S., but had been seen by
150,000,000 viewers in the Soviet Union. So much for the
impact of private enterprise. The President reiterated that
the government could not compel theatre owners to show films.
But he pointed to the recent visit of the Kirov ballet to
demonstrate that American audiences responded positively to
quality Soviet performers, and that Soviet culture did, in
fact, have access to the U.S. public.

Raising a final question in the "humanitarian" sphere,
Gorbachev complained that, for the past 30 years, the U.S. had
denied visas to Soviet trade union representatives seeking to
visit the United States. During the same period, many U.S.
labor leaders had visited the Soviet Union. Again, where was
the equality of access? The President agreed to look into the
matter as well as the question of what could be done with
respect to Soviet films.

The President said he had two additional points to raise.

First, he could not go back and tell the American farmers
that he had met with the General Secretary without raising the
Soviet failure to meet their obligations under the bilateral

- 20 -

Long Term Grain Agreement to buy the minimum amount of American wheat. Gorbachev replied that the President should tell them all the money the Russians had hoped to spend on grain was in America and Saudi Arabia as a result of lower oil prices. The President pointed out that America's oil industry had suffered as much as the Soviet Union's as a result of OPEC's pricing policies. We had had no hand in creating the hardships.

Second, the President wished to read a copy of a letter to Gorbachev from National Symphony Orchestra Director Rostropovich, seeking Gorbachev's approval for certain of Rostropovich's relatives to attend jubilee concerts in the West in connection with the maestro's 70th birthday. After the President read the letter, Gorbachev indicated that he had received it and responded personally, and that the necessary instructions had been given to enable Rostropovich's relatives to attend the celebrations. The President thanked Gorbachev.

Gorbachev noted that "the moment" appeared to have come.

Shevardnadze asked if he and the Secretary were to remain "unemployed," or if the leaders had any instructions for them.

The Secretary said he had tried to formulate some language on INF and space, recognizing that there had been agreement on the one hand, and a lack of agreement on the other. After being invited by Gorbachev to proceed, the Secretary read the following passage:

"The President and General Secretary discussed issues involving the ABM Treaty, advanced strategic defense, the relationship to ....? of offensive ballistic missiles intensively and at length. They will instruct their Geneva negotiators to use the record of these conversations to benefit their work."

Gorbachev said the statement was unacceptable, and asked that the passage on INF be read. The Secretary read the following passage:

....

Gorbachev said that that was clear. He suggested that, if the President had no objections, the two Foreign Ministers might see what they could come up with while the two leaders took a brief break. Gorbachev didn't mind waiting an hour or two.

- 21 -

Shevardnadze remarked that it should be possible to come
up with agreed language on nuclear testing. That would leave
the question of the duration of a non-withdrawal pledge with
respect to the ABM Treaty.

Gorbachev said that that had been covered in the
discussion. A withdrawal pledge was necessary to preserve and
strengthen the ABM Treaty so as to justify the risk of
reduction strategic and intermediate range offensive weapons.

Gorbachev proposed that, if the President agreed, the two
of them meet again at 3:00 pm. The President agreed, and
escorted Gorbachev from the room, ending the session.

CHRON FILE

United States Department of State

Washington, D.C. 20520   SYSTEM II
                               90725

MEMORANDUM OF CONVERSATION

DATE: October 12, 1986
TIME: 3:25 - 6:   PM
PLACE: Hofdi House, Reykjavik

PARTICIPANTS:

      U.S. Side   **Soviet Side**

   President Reagan   General Secretary Gorbachev
   Secretary Shultz   Foreign Minister Shevardnadze
   Tom Simons, Notetaker   P. Pavlazhchenko, Notetaker
   Dimitry Zarechnak,   Soviet Interpreter
    Interpreter

   <u>Gorbachev</u> asked whether the President wanted the Soviet
side to start, in which case he would have something to put on
the table. <u>The President</u> replied that it was Gorbachev's
choice.

   <u>Gorbachev</u> said that with regard to the ABM Treaty, the
Soviet side was introducing a proposal that takes into account
both the U.S. and Soviet positions, and links the process of
strengthening the ABM Treaty regime and the process of real
reductions in nuclear armaments. The proposal was as follows:

    The USSR and the United States undertake for ten years not
to exercise their existing right of withdrawal from the ABM
Treaty, which is of unlimited duration, and during that period
strictly to observe all its provisions. The testing in space
of all space components of anti-ballistic missile defense is
prohibited, except research and testing conducted in
laboratories. Within the first five years of the ten-year
period (and thus by the end of 1991), the strategic offensive
arms of the two sides shall be reduced by 50 percent. During
the following five years of that period, the remaining
50 percent of the two sides' strategic offensive arms shall be
reduced. Thus by the end of 1996, the strategic offensive arms
of the USSR and the United States will have been totally
eliminated.

   Gorbachev said this contained elements of both the Soviet
and the U.S. proposals. The Soviets were prepared to agree
that day to confirm the situation as it exists with the ABM
Treaty and to enrich it by the commitment to eliminate
strategic offensive weapons.

- 2 -

The President said this seemed only slightly different.
The Secretary noted that there were indeed differences.

The President said he has the following proposal.

Both sides would agree to confine themselves to research,
development and testing which is permitted by the ABM Treaty
for a period of five years, through 1991, during which time a
50% reduction in strategic offensive arsenals would be
achieved. This being done, both sides will continue the pace
of reductions with respect to all remaining offensive ballistic
missiles with the goal of the total elimination of all
offensive ballistic missiles by the end of a second five-year
period. As long as these reductions continue at the
appropriate pace, the same restrictions will continue to
apply. At the end of the ten-year period, with all offensive
ballistic missiles eliminated, either side would be free to
introduce defenses.

Gorbachev said his view was that the Soviets had moved
forward by adopting the periodization proposed by the U.S. --
two five-year periods -- while strengthening the ABM Treaty and
linking strengthening the ABM Treaty with reductions. With
regard to the U.S. side's formula, it does not move toward the
Soviet position. The Soviets' main objective, for the period
when we are pursuing deep reductions, is to strengthen the ABM
Treaty regime and not to undermine it. He would thus once
again ask the U.S. side to meet this minimal requirement.
Their proposal was intended to assure that today's ABM Treaty
is confirmed and strengthened, with secure obligations that for
ten years it will not be gone around, that there will be no
deployment of systems in space, as we go through deep
reductions to elimination of offensive weapons.

Gorbachev said he wanted to stress that the ban would not
be on research and testing in laboratories. They would be
confined to laboratories, but this would open opportunities for
both the U.S. and Soviet sides to do all the necessary research
in the field of space systems such as SDI. It would not
undermine SDI, but would put it in a certain framework. He
asked the President for an agreement that met these
requirements.

The President said that we had wanted to meet the Soviet
need for ten years, and we had done so. He asked why there
should be any restrictions beyond that period, when both sides
will have gotten what they claim they want -- the elimination
of offensive missiles. Why impose restrictions beyond the
ten-year period, he asked.

- 3 -

Gorbachev said this was not something that needed to be put down on paper.

The President said he did not see what the basic difference was, unless it was the interpretation of the Treaty.

Gorbachev said that with regard to his proposal he did not know why it could not be accepted. After ten years the two sides could find out what the solutions were through talks. The solution would not necessarily be SDI. The U.S. might find it was SDI, and the Soviets might find it was something else. He didn't see why we need to sign on blindly to SDI at this point. Thus the Soviets had come up with a formula that meets this: in the next several years after the ten-year period the two sides would find solutions in this field in negotiations. This was a broad formula that after ten years the U.S. could continue SDI if it wanted. If the U.S. wanted, this could be discussed in negotiations, after the ten years. Why pledge to SDI right now, he asked.

The President replied that he assumed both sides agreed that verification would assure that neither had ballistic missiles after the ten years. Is it necessary to pledge something to assure that, he asked. Someone might come along who wants to redevelop nuclear missiles.

Gorbachev said that at least it was the Soviet view that for ten years, while we proceed to the unique historical task of eliminating nuclear forces, we should strengthen the ABM Treaty regime. Why should we create other problems whose prospects are dim and whose consequences are unknown, that leave one side in doubt about reducing nuclear weapons while the other side retains them under the guise of defensive weapons. Why burden agreement by these weights? It was hard enough to come to this agreement. That is why they link reductions to doing without defensive systems for ten years. Afterwards we can discuss them. But during the ten years there should be only laboratory research. We can see what the situation is while we eliminate offensive weapons, and then discuss what next after that. It is comprehensible and logical to retain the Treaty. The U.S. side would be permitted laboratory research, and of course the Soviet side would too. In the U.S. case this would mean SDI. The Soviets were not trying to bury SDI.

The President said the Soviets had asked for ten years, and we had given ten and a half, because after ten years we would have to give the six-month withdrawal notice. During that period both sides would be able to do the research, development and testing which is permitted by the ABM Treaty.

- 4 -

If they then decide to go forward with defenses, what objection
can there be unless something is being hidden? This provides
protection for the future. We will make it available to the
Soviet side if it wants it.

If the Soviets felt that strongly about strengthening the
ABM Treaty, why didn't they get rid of Krasnoyarsk and the
whole defense structure they have built around their capital,
the President asked. They have a big defense structure and we
have none. It is a peculiar fact that we do not have a single
defense against a nuclear attack.

Gorbachev reiterated that what the Soviets said about
research and testing in the laboratory constituted the basis
and the opportunity for the U.S. to go on within the
frameworkof SDI. So the U.S. would not have renounced SDI on
its side. He was a convinced opponent of a situation where
there is a winner and a loser. In that case, after the
agreement is ratified, the loser would take steps to undermine
the agreement, so that could not be the right basis. There had
to be an equal footing. The documents should be deserving of
ratification as being in the interest of both sides.

The President asked what then is wrong with going by this
and then saying that the question of the research, development
and testing which is permitted by the ABM Treaty is reserved
for their meeting in Washington, that they then could decide
whether it is under the ABM provisions.

Gorbachev replied that without that there was no package.
He believed the Soviet side had convinced the U.S. side of the
existence of an interrelationship between the issues. If we
agree on deep reductions in nuclear weapons we need confidence
that the ABM Treaty will be observed during the period of the
process of eliminating them. This would be a very historic
period, improving a dangerous situation after a period of
tensions. This decision would also be in the interest of the
U.S. during that time.

The President commented that they were not getting
anyplace. He proposed they consider why there was an objection
to the U.S. formula if they agreed that ten years down the road
there would be no ballistic missiles. He proposed a recess
where they would meet with their people, and see what is
keeping them apart.

After the break, the President presented a revised
proposal for agreement. The proposal was as follows:

- 5 -

The USSR and the United States undertake for ten years not to exercise their existing right of withdrawal from the ABM Treaty, which is of unlimited duration, and during that period strictly to observe all its provisions. Within the first five years of the ten-year period (and thus by the end of 1991), the strategic offensive arms of the two sides shall be reduced by 50 percent. During the following five years of that period, the strategic offensive arms of the two sides shall be reduced. Thus by the end of 1996, the strategic offensive arms of the USSR and the United States will have been eliminated. At the end of the ten-year period, either side could deploy defenses if it so chose, provided the two sides did not agree otherwise.

The President said Secretary Shultz would explain the differences. The Secretary said the addition drew on paragraph 3 of the previous day's paper. He went on to say there seemed to be two differences. The first is how to handle what is permitted during the ten years. The second, if he understood correctly, is that the Soviets see a period of indefinite duration for agreement not to depart from the ABM Treaty, while the U.S. side sees ten years.

Gorbachev said we needed clarity at this stage about whether to undertake real reductions while strengthening, not weakening, the ABM Treaty regime. Thus, the right to withdraw that both sides have now would not be used for ten years, and after ten years we would consider how to deal with the question. Perhaps we would keep to it, perhaps there would be new elements. But in those ten years we would strengthen and not weaken the Treaty regime.

The Secretary asked whether Gorbachev was saying that after ten years the aspect about not withdrawing would also be over. Gorbachev replied that after ten years the two sides could exercise all sorts of rights. The Secretary commented that that helped. Gorbachev suggested they add to the text the sentence "In the course of the succeeding several years, the two sides should find in the course of negotiations further mutually acceptable solutions in this field." Shevardnadze commented that under the Soviet proposal there would be no limit on research, except that it would be confined to laboratories.

Gorbachev asked the President to recall their meeting in Geneva. The President was host; tt was on the last night; they were sitting on the sofa drinking coffee. They were in a good atmosphere. At that point Shultz came in to report that the Soviet delegation did not agree on certain points. The President had asked him, sitting there on the sofa, what the hell should be done, and suggested banging his hand on the

- 6 -

table. He had gone out, and in fifteen minutes everything was
fixed. Now they could go out in the same way, and fix
everything in ten minutes. It would be another victory for the
U.S. side.

The Secretary said he wanted to be clear about one thing.
The Soviet proposal said that during the second five-year
period the remaining weapons would be "reduced." Did "reduced"
mean at a constant pace? Gorbachev said that the modalities
could be written down in the treaty. The Secretary noted that
the question was referred to when the President talked about
strategic offensive weapons.

Gorbachev recalled that the day before the Soviets had
proposed that all components be cut by half. This was for the
first five years. It covered the whole triad. The second half
would take care of the rest.

The Secretary noted that our proposal referred to
"offensive ballistic missiles," and the Soviet to "strategic
offensive arms." These may be different categories. He wanted
to be sure.

Gorbachev repeated that the Soviets had made a proposal
the day before. He could say frankly it had not been a easy
decision. If we try to search for levels, subceilings, we will
never get out of it. He had suggested that they cut through
this, and cut everything by 50%, including the SS-18s the U.S.
was concerned about. Other missiles which were not strategic
would be covered by the separate agreements that have been made.

The President and the General Secretary agreed to take
another break.

After the break, the President said he had been sorry to
keep Gorbachev so long, but Gorbachev knew the trouble
Americans had getting along with each other.

The President continued that he had spent this long time
trying very hard to meet the General Secretary's desire for a
ten-year situation. This had to be his final effort.
The President then read the following text:

The USSR and the United States undertake for ten years not
to exercise their existing right of withdrawal from the ABM
Treaty, which is of unlimited duration, and during that period
strictly to observe all its provisions, while continuing
research, development and testing which is permitted by the ABM

- 7 -

Treaty. Within the first five years of the ten-year period
(and thus through 1991), the strategic offensive arms of the
two sides shall be reduced by 50 percent. During the following
five years of that period, the remaining 50 percent of the two
sides' offensive ballistic missiles shall be reduced. Thus by
the end of 1996, all offensive ballistic missiles of the USSR
and the United States will have been totally eliminated.

Gorbachev referred to the text of "research, development
and testing which is permitted by the ABM Treaty," and noted
that reference to laboratory testing had disappeared. The
President replied that instead the Soviet side now had the line
about research, development and testing which is permitted by
the ABM Treaty.

Gorbachev asked what the purpose of this was. The
President replied that their people in Geneva must decide what
is permitted. The two sides have different views on this.

Gorbachev asked again whether the language on laboratory
testing had been omitted on purpose. He was trying to clarify
the U.S. proposal.

Gorbachev continued that his next question was that the
first part of the proposal talks about strategic offensive
weapons, and the second part about ballistic missiles. He
asked why there is this difference of approach.

The President said he had received the message while he
was upstairs that the Soviets were mainly interested in
ballistic missiles. He had thought earlier that they were
thinking of everything nuclear, and then he had heard it was
ballistic missiles.

Gorbachev said no, they had in mind strategic offensive
weapons. He then turned to medium-range missiles.

The President interrupted to ask what Gorbachev meant.

Gorbachev said he could confirm that the Soviets are for
reducing strategic offensive weapons. Other agreements would
cover other weapons, for instance medium-range weapons. That
part on what the U.S. side called INF is in paragraph 2 of the
draft. There we would also deal with missiles with ranges of
less than 1000 kilometers. He was not removing anything from
the table, but he wanted to be sure there is identity in the
two parts. He was not changing positions. He wished to
clarify things.

The President proposed to add "strategic" to our language,
making it "strategic offensive ballistic missiles."

- 8 -

Gorbachev asked where aircraft were. They were in the triad, and we had agreed to reduce the whole triad: land-based strategic missiles, sea-launched, strategic bombers. The two sides had determined long ago what is strategic.

The President said we had proposed reducing all ballistic missiles on land and sea, but he was ready to include all the nuclear weapons we can.

Gorbachev said we should use the whole triad.

The President said then we should take out "strategic." Then all ballistic missiles would be eliminated.

Gorbachev said we should include land-based, sea-based and bombers.

The President asked if that were the only thing Gorbachev objected to in the U.S. proposal.

Gorbachev said he was just clarifying to be sure. He would explain the Soviet position.

The President said if this was a problem we should work on it. We had agreed to the record of the group on reducing all three elements.

Gorbachev said the agreement should be identical for both sides, for the first and second five-year periods. The concept is to reduce 50% for all types. At the same time they had agreed to the American rule, taking into account gravity bombs and SRAMs.

The President said there had been a misunderstanding on our part as to what the Soviets wanted.

The Secretary said he thought we had to be careful when it came to eliminating all strategic offensive arms if we don't deal with short-range ballistic missiles. He realized we were dealing with it in another place, but perhaps this was the place to deal with it decisively.
Gorbachev said Shultz could write into the text on the second period that all strategic offensive arms will have been eliminated, "including ballistic missiles." The missiles with ranges shorter than 1000 kilometers are handled in the medium-range agreement. We should write we will freeze them and then negotiate about their destruction. Everything should be encompassed. Missiles of less than 1000 kilometers are being handled elsewhere. Freeze them and then start talks about their destruction.

- 9 -

The Secretary said we are talking about two stages, the first five years and the second five years. Insofar as we deal with intermediate- and short-range weapons, we talked about an agreement to last until it was superseded. But we think of this as a first tranche. Gorbachev asked what that meant. The Secretary said it meant a first batch. Presumably, he continued, what we have agreed to on INF will happen within the first five years. All the missiles will be gone.

Gorbachev said yes, including those with less than 1000 kilometers' range as well. But when you speak about ABM you speak only about strategic weapons. We have a common understanding about what is strategic.

The Secretary commented that the treaty is about anti-ballistic missiles. These are not only strategic. He recognized there may not be much of an argument here.

Gorbachev said he did not think there was a difference between the two sides.

The Secretary suggested that if we add "and all offensive ballistic missiles," we can come to closure.

Gorbachev asked again why it is different for the two periods. In the first paragraph we speak of strategic offensive arms. He did not think there had to be this contradistinction. We can sort that out when we do the paper.

The President agreed this could be sorted out. He asked whether Gorbachev was saying that beginning in the first five-year period and then going on in the second we would be reducing all nuclear weapons -- cruise missiles, battlefield weapons, sub-launched and the like. It would be fine with him if we eliminated all nuclear weapons.

Gorbachev said we can do that. We can eliminate them.

The Secretary said, "Let's do it."

The President reiterated that he had thought he had gotten a message that Gorbachev was interested mainly in ballistic missiles. Gorbachev reiterated that there is a contradiction in the first and second periods. In the first it is all strategic offensive weapons, in the second only one type of arms, and that leaves the rest out.

The President said that if they could agree to eliminate all nuclear weapons, he thought they could turn it over to their Geneva people with that understanding, for them to draft

- 10 -

up that agreement, and Gorbachev could come to the U.S. and
sign it.

Gorbachev agreed. He continued that he now wanted to turn
to the ABM Treaty. He was apprehensive about this. If the
treaty is of unlimited duration, and there is to be strict
observance of its provisions, and the two sides agree not to
use their right to withdraw, then it is incomprehensible why
research, development and testing should go on and not be
confined to the laboratory. The U.S. evidently saw the Treaty
otherwise. We should add to its strength.

We will be proceeding on to a broad reduction of offensive
weapons, Gorbachev continued. This would allow for research
and testing in laboratories but not elsewhere. Otherwise one
side could do research, development and testing anywhere, while
pretending it is not violating the ABM Treaty. This would give
the impression that one side was trying to create an unequal
situation. He liked to be clear. He wanted to have
laboratory-only in. The Soviet side is for strict observance
of the Treaty, and only laboratory research and testing. He
could not do without the word "laboratory." If the U.S. side
was indeed for strict observance, it should also be for
"laboratory."

The President said that from the beginning of the Treaty
there had been this difference. There was a sort of liberal
interpretation, and also one that confined this strictly to
laboratories. This was a legitimate difference. But we had
gone a long way, and what the hell difference did it make. Ten
years down the road some country might come along with a madman
who wanted to build nuclear weapons again.

The President said they could be proud of what they had
done. We may not build SDI in the end; it might be too
expensive, for instance. But he had promised the American
people he would not give up SDI. The Soviets now had ten
years. We have an agreement we can be very proud of.

Gorbachev asked whether the U.S. side would not have the
right to decide on SDI development if it put in that it
recognized that work would go on only in laboratories,
including SDI-related work. But he had to take a principled
position that the work could only be in laboratories. This
would mean it could not be transferred outside, to create
weapons and put them in space. That was why strict observance
meant confining work to laboratories. If the President agreed,
they could write that down, and sign now.

- 11 -

The President said that Gorbachev talked about deployment as if it meant weapons in space. We already had agreements that prevented that. He thought the Soviets were violating agreements. There is the Krasnoyarsk radar. They should knock it down.

Gorbachev said the U.S. might be testing objects, and say they were not offensive, but there would be suspicions. The Soviet side said testing should take place only in laboratories.

The President said he would not destroy the possibility of proceeding with SDI. He could not confine work to the laboratory.

Gorbachev said he understood this was the President's final position. He could not confine work to the laboratory.

The President said, "Yes." We have said we will do what we do within what we believe are within the limits of the Treaty. But there is disagreement as to what the Treaty proscribes.

Gorbachev said he understood the U.S. wanted a concrete formula that gives the U.S. the possibility of conducting tests not only in the laboratory but outside, and in space.

The President said there is research in the lab stage, but then you must go outdoors to try out what has been done in the lab.

Gorbachev suggested that they write in "experimental." This includes mockups, prototypes, samples. But they needed to write "only in laboratories."

Gorbachev continued that he was not saying what he was saying to be intransigent, or rigid, or casuistical. He was being very serious. If they were going to agree to deep reductions in nuclear weapons, and the U.S. side wanted an interpretation that allowed it to conduct all sorts of research that would go against the ABM Treaty, and put weapons in space and build a large-scale defense system, then this was unacceptable. But if the U.S. agreed to confine this work to laboratories, the Soviet side would sign. That was why in their draft tests of all space elements in space were banned, except for laboratory work.

The President said he could not give in.

Gorbachev said that was the last word.

- 12 -

The President said he had a problem in his country
Gorbachev did not have. If they criticized Gorbachev, they
went to jail. (Gorbachev interjected during the interpretation
that the President should read some of the things being written
in Soviet newspapers.) But, the President continued, he had
people who were the most outspoken critics of the Soviet Union
over the years, the so-called right wing, an esteemed
journalist, who were the first to criticize him. They were
kicking his brains out.

Gorbachev would go home with the ten years, the President
went on. He himself would go home with his pledge to stick by
SDI, and continue research within our interpretation of the ABM
Treaty when it came to research. He was not asking anything
unusual.

Addressing the President, Gorbachev said he assumed the
President was addressing him from a position of equality, in
another country, on a confidential basis, and he would thus be
frank.

The President was three steps away from becoming a great
President, Gorbachev said, if they signed what had been
discussed and agreed to. These would be very major steps. But
they needed to include strict observance of the ABM Treaty and
confinement of research and testing to laboratories, including
SDI-related work.

But if this was not possible, they could say goodbye, and
forget everything they had discussed. What had been discussed
here in Reykjavik was a last opportunity, at least for
Gorbachev.

He had had the firm belief when he came here -- and
otherwise he would not have proposed the meeting -- that the
proposals of the Soviet Union, of the Soviet leadership, were
very far-reaching, and built on a huge reservoir of
constructive spirit. With the support of the U.S. side, they
could solve very important problems.

If they were able to do this, Gorbachev continued, and
resolve these problems, all the President's critics would not
open their mouths. The peoples of the U.S., of the Soviet
Union, of the whole world would cheer. Now, if he (Gorbachev)
saw that the President could not agree to these proposals, the
people would say that the political leaders could not agree.
What they had discussed would be left for another generation.

Gorbachev continued that the President had not made a
single, substantial, major step in Gorbachev's direction.

SECRET/SENSITIVE
- 13 -

Shevardnadze said he wanted to say just one thing. The
two sides were so close to accomplishing a historic task, to
decisions of such historic significance, that if future
generations read the minutes of these meetings, and saw how
close we had come but how we did not use these opportunities,
they would never forgive us.

The President said he wished to speak as one political
leader to another political leader. He had a problem of great
importance to him on this particular thing. He had been
attacked even before he came. He had given up a long span of
time. He was asking Gorbachev, as a political leader, to do
this one thing to make it possible for him to deal with
Gorbachev in the future. If he did what Gorbachev asked, he
would be badly hurt in his own country. He asked this one
thing of Gorbachev.

Gorbachev said he had said everything he had to say, just
as the President had.

The President asked Gorbachev to listen once again to what
he had proposed: "during that period strictly to observe all
its provisions, while continuing research, testing and
development which is permitted by the ABM Treaty." It is a
question of one word. This should not be turned down over a
word. Anyone reading that would believe that the U.S. is
committed to the ABM Treaty.

Gorbachev commented that he could also say the President
was using one word to frustrate a meeting that had promised to
be historic. But he would speak seriously. It is not just a
question of a word, but a question of principle. If we are to
agree to deep reductions and elimination of nuclear weapons, we
must have a firm footing, a front and rear that we can rely
on. But if the Soviet side signed something that gave the U.S.
the opportunity to conduct SDI-related research and testing in
broad tests, and to go into space, the testing of space weapons
in space, he could not return to Moscow. He could not go back
and say we are going to start reductions, and the U.S. will
continue to do research, testing and development that will
allow it to create weapons and a large-scale space defense
system in ten years.

If we say research and testing in laboratories, he could
sign it, Gorbachev went on. But if he went back and said that
research, testing and development could go on outside the
laboratory and the system could go ahead in ten years, he would
be called a dummy (durak) and not a leader. Ten years of
research in the laboratories within the limits of the Treaty
ought to be enough for the President. He was not against SDI.
But the research had to be in the laboratories.

SECRET/SENSITIVE

- 14 -

The President said he had believed, and had said so in
Geneva, that he and Gorbachev had the possibility of getting
along as no two American and Soviet leaders ever had before.
He had asked Gorbachev for a favor, which was important to him
and to what he could do with Gorbachev in the future.
Gorbachev had refused him that favor.

Gorbachev replied that if the President had come to him
and said things are hard for American farmers, and asked him to
buy some American grain, he would have understood. But what
the President was asking him to agree to on behalf of the USSR
was to allow the U.S. -- at a time when they were proceeding to
deep reductions and elimination of nuclear weapons -- to
conduct full-scale research and development, including
development of a space-based ABM system, which would permit the
U.S. to destroy the Soviet Union's offensive nuclear
potential. The President would not like it if Gorbachev had
asked that of him. It would cause nervousness and suspicion.
It was not an acceptable request. It could not be met. The
President was not asking for a favor, but for giving up a point
of principle.

The President said there would be no offensive weapons
left to destroy, and space defenses could not be deployed for
ten years or so. It was not the word, it was the implication.
Gorbachev was asking him to give up the thing he'd promised not
to give up. All the other language was what Gorbachev had
needed. We had said we would comply with the Treaty for ten
years. It is the particular meaning of one word. Gorbachev
knew how this would be taken in the U.S.

The President continued that if Gorbachev thought the
problem was that he wanted some military advantage, Gorbachev
should not worry. He did not talk about it much, but he
believed the Soviets were violating the ABM Treaty. He was not
saying we should tear it down, and we should say nothing
outside this room, but we should not stop at one word. The
President had met Gorbachev's requirements. What more was
needed than that?

The President said he was asking Gorbachev to change his
mind as a favor to him, so that hopefully they could go on and
bring peace to the world.

Gorbachev said he could not do it. If they could agree to
ban research in space, he would sign in two minutes. They
should add to the text "The testing in space of all space
components of missile defense is prohibited, except research
and testing conducted in laboratories," as in the draft. The
point was not one of words, but of principle.

- 15 -

He would like to move everywhere he could.   He had tried
to do so.   His conscience was clear before the President and
his people.   What had depended on him he had done.

Prepared by: TWSimons, Jr.
            10/14/86

Appendix Two

Implications of the
Reykjavik Summit on
Its Twentieth Anniversary

October 10–12, 2006
Hoover Institution
Stanford University
Stanford, California

AGENDA

Tuesday, October 10
6:00 P.M.   Informal gathering and dinner

Wednesday, October 11
8:00 A.M.   Continental Breakfast
8:30 A.M.   Welcoming Remarks by Director John Raisian,
             Hoover Institution
8:35 A.M.   **Session I: The Reykjavik Summit**

             Discussion Leader: George P. Shultz
             This session will review this historic event,
             including:
             • The build up to and preparations for the Summit.
             • The agenda and what happened as a result,
               including its impact in Moscow and Washington,
               and on arms control, human rights, bilateral and
               regional issues.
             Speakers: Rozanne Ridgway, Richard Perle, Roald
             Sagdeev, Don Oberdorfer, and Max Kampelman
12:00 P.M.   Lunch
12:45 P.M.   *Recalling Ronald Reagan's View of Nuclear Weapons*
             Presented by Martin Anderson

1:30 P.M.   **Session II: The Legacy of Reykjavik**

Discussion Leader: Sidney Drell

This session will focus on the major changes in political/strategic factors over the past two decades:

- The roles and missions of nuclear weapons, offensive and defensive systems, and prospects for nuclear nonproliferation and the NPT.

- Progress on human rights, bilateral U.S.-Russian relations, and dealing with regional issues.

- The spread of technology to newly emerging nations; and the intertwining of nuclear technology for civilian power and economic development with that for weapons, which presents serious intelligence challenges, and is making the nonproliferation regime more difficult to preserve.

- The rise of terrorism seeking nuclear weapons, the growing cooperation among the nuclear powers against the terrorist threats, and the role of international organizations and controls on nuclear fuel.

This discussion will be structured around specific national programs or geographic regions (i.e. North Korea, India and South Asia, Iran and the Middle East), focusing on how Reagan's ideas about nuclear weapons affected the way those changes were addressed or whether his ideas were not pursued by his successors as they faced new challenges.

5:00 P.M.   Adjourn

RECEPTION & DINNER

6:30 P.M.   Reception

7:00 P.M.   Panel Discussion
- George P. Shultz
- Max Kampelman
- Rozanne Ridgway
- Peter Robinson, moderator

8:00 P.M.   Dinner

9:30 p.m.   Adjourn

Thursday, October 12

8:00 A.M.   Continental Breakfast

8:30 A.M.   **Session III: Realizing the Vision of Ronald Reagan and Mikhail Gorbachev**

Discussion Leaders:
George Shultz and Sidney Drell

This session will attempt to formulate practical steps to surmount diplomatic and intelligence barriers to making progress toward further reductions in nuclear weaponry, assuring nonproliferation, and ultimately achieving a world free of nuclear weapons.

12:00 P.M.   Adjourn and Breakaway Lunch

Participants
Reykjavik I Conference
Martin Anderson
Steve Andreasen
Michael Armacost
Admiral William Crowe
Sidney Drell
James Goodby
Thomas Graham
Thomas Henriksen
David Holloway
Max Kampelman
Jack Matlock
John McLaughlin
Don Oberdorfer
Richard Perle
William Perry
Peter Robinson
Harry Rowen
Scott Sagan
Roald Sagdeev
George Shultz
Abe Sofaer
James Timbie

Related Pre-conference Publications

*Pre-conference publications on related topics
by conference participants:*

Andreasen, Steve. "Reagan Was Right: Let's Ban Ballistic Missiles," in *SURVIVAL: The IISS Quarterly* (published by the International Institute for Strategic Studies), Vol. 46, No. 1, Spring 2004.

Drell, Sidney D., and James E. Goodby. *The Gravest Danger: Nuclear Proliferation.* Stanford, Calif.: Hoover Institution Press, 2003. (Includes Foreword by George P. Shultz.)

Drell, Sidney D., and James E. Goodby. *What Are Nuclear Weapons For? Recommendations for Restructuring U.S. Strategic Forces*, An Arms Control Association Report. Washington, DC: Arms Control Association, April 2005.

Graham, Thomas, Jr. "Sixty Years After Hiroshima, A New Nuclear Era," *Current History*, Vol. 104, No. 681, April 2005.

Graham, Thomas, Jr. *Commonsense on Weapons of Mass Destruction.* Seattle: University of Washington Press, 2004.

Kampelman, Max. "Bombs Away," *New York Times*, April 24, 2006.

Kampelman, Max. "A Serious Look at Our World," *Vital Speeches of the Day*, Vol. LXXII, No.16–17, June 2006.

Perry, William J. "Proliferation on the Peninsula: Five North Korean Nuclear Crises," in *Confronting the Specter of Nuclear Terrorism*, The ANNALS of the American Academy of Political and Social Science, September 2006. Vol. 607: 78–86. Thousand Oaks, Calif.: Sage Publications, 2006.

Index